Happy Kids, Happy Dogs

Building a Friendship
Right from the Start

Barbara Shumannfang

Happy Kids, Happy Dogs

Building a Friendship Right from the Start

Barbara Shumannfang

ISBN 10: 1-4116-7212-7
ISBN 13: 978-1-4116-7212-3

Acknowledgements

It took a lot of people and dogs to make this book possible. I'd like to thank Justin Faerber, my editor, for the many ways in which he improved the manuscript. I am grateful to David Spratte for bringing the book to life with his extraordinary design talents.

I offer huge thanks to my clients who so generously contributed photos of their two-legged and four-legged family members, especially Hannah Arps and Blythe Dyson, Lisa Gehtland, Celeste Huntington, and Ginger Long. I thank Colony Park Animal Hospital for allowing me to photograph their staff and patients. Special thanks to Dr. Susanne Hughes, Dr. Christine Kapp and Dr. Alison Klaitman for their advice on pre-baby veterinary exams.

I was very lucky to have feedback from a group of knowledgeable and insightful readers including Katy Bartlett, Dee Ganley, Virginia Hoffman, Suzy Hughes and Janice Lynn Triptow. Their helpful suggestions and enthusiasm for the project made it a real pleasure to complete.

Most special thanks go to Dave for all the ways he's made creating this book, and everything else, splendido.

Table of Contents

Chapter 3: Your Growing and Changing Child

Chapter 4: The Other Dogs in Your Child's Life

Conclusion

Introduction:
Protect Your Child, Protect Your Dog

A Little Girl and a Big Dog

One day a young couple and their toddler went to visit a friend. The mom was somewhat worried, because the friend had a very large dog who had growled at strangers before, but the parents decided to make the visit and asked the friend to keep the dog away. Soon it was nap time, so the parents nestled the little girl in the guest room. She napped for a while as the grown-ups talked, but eventually she became restless. Although the toddler had only recently learned to walk, she was very curious and quite sure on her feet. Unbeknownst to the adults, she decided to leave the guest room and somehow she found her way to the kitchen where the dog was enjoying a bone. The adults heard a low, loud growl from the kitchen. The dad leapt to his feet. Just as the dog lunged at the child, the dad appeared in the kitchen doorway and scooped up the child. The dog's teeth sunk into the dad's thigh instead of the little girl's face. Years later the once little girl thanked her dad for helping her avoid a close call. That little girl was me.

Now that I am grown and my job is to help people with their dogs, I have come to learn that my childhood story is all too common. There are many close calls, plenty of bites, and mobile children are at greatest risk. According to the Centers for Disease Control and Prevention, each year there are about 4.7 million dog bites reported in emergency rooms. This number does not include the unknown number of bites treated at home, by a family physician, or by an urgent care center. The majority of bites are not to animal professionals or postal workers, but to children —more than 60 percent. And here is the kicker: The vast majority of dog bites are not delivered by an unknown dog that suddenly appears out of an alley. Rather, about 80 percent of dog bites are delivered by the family dog or a neighbor's dog.

A dog bite is something we want to prevent, because it causes stress and injury to the child, and often puts the dog's fate in jeopardy.

Given how many dogs live with people without biting (there are about 74 million companion dogs in the United States), one could reasonably argue that 4.7 million is not really a large number of dog bites. However, given that children are at such particularly high risk, with bites treated in emergency rooms most often sustained to the head and face, it makes sense to take reasonable precautions to avoid this happening to them. In other words, although lightning rarely strikes a person, that does not mean you would be cavalier about your child standing under a tall tree during a thunderstorm.

Another consideration is the climate for lawsuits in this country. In 2003, the Insurance Information Institute estimated that dog bites accounted for 25 percent of all home-owner's insurance claims. When you consider that staggering statistic along with the fact that most dog bites occur at home, you realize that a dog bite to a child visiting your home could put you at risk for a lawsuit, higher insurance payments, or even cancellation of your home-owner's insurance. Although you may consider such measures an overreaction to incidents that would not have warranted such consequences when you were growing up, times have changed, and it's not a good time to leave child-dog interactions to chance.

Myths and Reality about Dogs and Kids

When I talk with parents about promoting safe child-dog interactions, I am struck by the many common misconceptions parents have. There are many popular but mythical notions about dogs and children that can get both in trouble. Each of these well-meaning notions has some basis in reality, but it is important to recognize that most of these assumptions are not based on sound information and could put your child or dog at risk.

"I'd like it if my dog would be our child's protector."

It is best indeed if the child and dog are allies, but to imagine that your dog should be your child's protector is to make some dangerous assumptions. First, relying on your dog to protect your child implies that you are not around to do so. This is very risky. Your child and dog should never be left alone together. Period. Second, your dog cannot, and should not be expected to, make decisions as to what is best for your child's welfare. That is the job of a parent or an adult guardian. Dogs have proven cognitive abilities, but testing them out on your child is not responsible. Put another way, Lassie was a movie actor, and in real life would just as soon have rolled around on a dead squirrel as shown up barking to announce that Timmy had fallen in the well. Finally, does it really seem wise to risk having your dog make decisions about which people need to be threatened or harmed, and which need to be welcomed? Your dog may decide to "protect" your child from adults or other children who are friends. Most people agree that the risks of injury and lawsuits from this kind of dog behavior really aren't worth it.

"Now that we're having a baby, we'll probably have to get rid of the dog."

It is a good sign that you want to protect your child. This is part of your job as a parent. However, be sure to think through such a big decision carefully. If you think you need to find a new home for your dog, on what are you basing this assumption? Are you worried the dog will be jealous? What reason do you have to think the dog will be a threat to your baby? Are you afraid you won't have time to take care of the dog once the baby comes? Perhaps you're concerned about germs and disease prevention.

Whatever your concerns, it is very important to go beyond the well-meaning, but not necessarily up-to-date, information offered by friends, family, and even health care providers who may not be dog specialists. Your dog's future is at stake, so it is important that you not rush into anything based on uninformed advice. While it is possible that you may need to find another home for your dog, it is essential that you first seek out reliable information. Each of the above concerns will be addressed in this book. There are resources in the appendix so that you can get further assistance if you need it.

"You can do anything to our dog and he doesn't mind at all."

Certainly it is important to have a dog that seeks out human touch and who seems eager to take it in all its forms. This is especially true where the safety of children is concerned. The trouble with assuming that "the dog is fine" with any type of handling is this: in all my work with parents and dogs, I have never heard of a dog owner basing this assumption on information that the dog is giving them. Instead, they base the assumption that "the dog is fine" on a combination of their own desire to have such a fairy tale type of dog and the fact that the dog has simply not yet bitten anyone.

There are some things that are not okay to do to any dog—not just to avoid a bite, but out of respect for the dog. Many times children touch dogs in inappropriate ways that cause the dog's stress level to build. The dog then gives many subtle warning signs to show that the child is applying too much stress. This book will teach you how to recognize those warning signs and what they mean, and what to do when you see them. We can choose to ignore those signs (and then claim the bite event just "came out of the blue") or we can learn to read the signs, protect our child and our dog, and teach our child about respecting others. We expect a lot from our dogs. I think it's only fair to meet them half way. That's the sort of respect and empathy most parents want to demonstrate to their children.

"I supervise my child and dog, so I know they're fine."

This is an excellent concept, but one that is usually misapplied. A few years ago I began to notice this when my clients would discuss a concern about their dog's behavior toward their child. They would begin by saying they always supervise the child and dog. Naturally I was always very impressed and relieved to hear this. Yet here they were, seeking out my help because of something that had gone wrong between the dog and the child. How could things be going wrong if the parents were supervising?

Here's the pattern I noticed: As the parent told the story of the growl or the bite event, phrases would pop out like, "So when I heard the noise, I went into the room and saw that the dog had. . . " or, "We were all out in the yard, and when I looked over I saw Johnny. . ." Eureka. The source of the misunderstanding was clear. "Supervision" as most parents use the term in regards to children is not adequate for monitoring child-dog interactions. When it comes to your child and your dog, good old fashioned supervision just doesn't cut it. Fortunately there is something much more effective you can do instead. I call it being a kid canine coach, and this book will teach you how.

Why Dog-Friendly Training Is Important for Your Child

Have you noticed how quickly your dog can form associations you didn't even teach on purpose? For example, when you pick up the leash, he feels so happy he makes a complete loon of himself. Or maybe when you prepare his dinner, he dances around with glee. Did you intentionally teach him to feel that way? Probably not. And yet it took only a repetition or two for him to learn "Leash=good!" or "Food bag rustling sound=good!"

Now think about your child, and the associations you want your dog to make with him or her. If in the past you trained your dog using collar corrections or verbal reprimands like a harsh "No!" you may have gotten the results you wanted in terms of training. However, I strongly recommend you not use pain or intimidation to teach your dog manners if you plan to have a child in your household. If your child is nearby, your dog may readily associate your child with the pain or unpleasant sensation of a collar correction, the fear experienced with yelling or threats, or the dread that wells up at the sight of a spray bottle. For your child's safety and for the sake of a trusting relationship between child and dog, we want your dog to learn "Child=good!" so it's important to create pleasant associations.

These two are making a pleasant association with each other; the child offers a treat and the dog takes it gently.
Photo courtesy of Celeste Huntington.

The right training treat

For best results, use treats that are soft, do not crumble when broken, and are no larger than a pea (or smaller for tiny dogs). Let your dog be the guide as to which treats she finds most delicious. A low-value reward would likely be pieces of her dog food. A medium-value treat would be Zuke's Mini Naturals brand soft treats or macaroni noodles you've cooked in broth instead of water. Very special, high-value treats will be called for at times in this book. Most dogs consider cheese, tofu dogs, real meat, or bits of fish to be very special rewards. Used in tiny amounts and never directly from the table, such high-value training treats are effective without affecting most dogs' health and table manners.

Luckily modern dog training makes this easy. You can create boundaries, discipline your dog, and teach new things without the use of older methods that may have relied on pain or fear to change your dog's behavior. This book will show you modern, dog-friendly approaches to training. Dog-friendly training means preventing behaviors you don't like and teaching and rewarding behaviors that you do like.

One of the most powerful ways to reward your dog, and to create pleasant associations with your child, is with food. The key to success is to have a plan and to use the rewards thoughtfully, so that the dog is actually learning rather than just being bribed. Bribery is not the most effective way to teach. In fact, some people bribe the dog so much that he cannot perform unless food is visible (the old "he won't do the trick unless I have a treat" syndrome). However, food used correctly, as a carefully timed reward, can produce fast, solid results without spoiling your dog. In addition to food rewards, this book will show you how to enhance your dog's learning with the correct use of real-life rewards, such as leash walks and attention from you. That way you'll be able to reward your dog with many things in addition to food treats. I recommend dog-friendly training that involves food in addition to other rewards, because when it comes to the well-being of your child and your dog, it's best to go with methods that make your dog feel happy.

How to Use This Book to Set Up for Success

Kids are the most commonly bitten people, and bites are most commonly delivered by the family dog or a friend's dog. Therefore, the first purpose of this book is to help you prevent injury to your child. A nice bonus is that aiming for that goal will likely decrease stress for everyone in your household, including you and your dog.

The second purpose is to help you avoid guilt or worry. You probably care a great deal about your dog. Your dog may even be considered part of your family. So you may be concerned about how the dog will feel with a new, little person in the house who needs you so much. As your baby joins your family and grows, there will be many wonderful, unexpected, exciting changes in your life. A little preparation and knowledge can help make the doggie aspects of the transition flow much more smoothly. With the right information and preparation, you will worry less and feel less guilty about how your relationship with your dog will change.

The third purpose of this book is to help you create a good relationship between your child and your dog. It is important to teach your child how to be respectful and compassionate toward your dog, and to teach your dog to welcome your child as part of the family. Supervision alone does not accomplish this. What is required is so much more.

An affectionate moment caught on film (notice the little smile forming on the child's lips). These two will be playing fetch together in a few years. Photo by Jabrina Robinson.

Parents need to do three important things. They must actively coach the child, they must teach the dog to have a positive association with the child, and they must monitor dog stress and warning signs to gauge precisely how well the interactions are going. These three things are what contribute to a harmonious relationship between child and dog. As complex as it sounds at first, this book will provide you with simple, how-to guidelines.

The most wonderful desire that parents express over and over to me is the following: "I'd like my child and dog to be friends."

Friends care about each other, help each other, respect each other and can count on each other. They share sad times and happy times, and they teach each other things. They listen and they try to understand each other. Friends can trust each other. With the right guidance from parents, children and their dogs can have wonderful friendships.

Chapter 1:
Preparing for Baby

Can You Keep Your Dog?

Parents seem to fall into two categories when it comes to this question. Most parents simply assume their child and dog will be fine together, without really thinking through how to actively achieve this result. Some of these parents are so sure their dog is "fine" that they put their child and their dog in risky situations. Other parents go to the opposite extreme. They assume they cannot keep their dog because they are having a baby.

In short, many decisions about keeping or giving up your dog are based on misinformation and half-truths. Your child and your dog are both very important to you, so I recommend stepping back and, as objectively as possible, carefully thinking through the decision about whether or not to keep your dog.

Consider the facts about your dog's past behavior

Most people assume their dog likes children if the dog has never growled at or bitten a child. In fact, many people insist that their dog loves children, simply because they strongly want to believe that their dog loves children. I'll give you a typical example. One client visited me with her small dog. We were discussing an obedience training issue when my neighbor's child came out into his backyard, which adjoined my training area. The boy, who was about eleven years old, was getting ready to play catch with his dad. Slowly my client's dog left us and made his way over to the fence where the child was. Bursting with pride, the dog's owner said, "Oh, he just loves children!" That surprised me because there was nothing in the dog's body language to indicate he was glad to see the boy. The dog was very stiff, and stared silently at the boy through the fence. We moved toward the dog. When we were about 30 feet away, I noticed the dog's pattern of respiration change. He was growling. I said to the owner, "Really? He loves children?

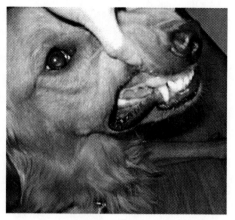

All dogs have teeth, and any dog can bite under circumstances he or she perceives as threatening or stressful.
Photos by author.

And what makes you say that?" "Oh," she said, "he has just always loved children." Naturally, I then invited her to examine the dog's body language. A dog who stands stiffly, staring at a child, with his center of gravity forward, emitting a low growl is not showing pleasure at the sight of the child. Does your dog see a child and begin to get wiggly, trying to approach the child with a low, wagging tail and squinty eyes? Dogs who love kids get a little giddy when they see them and actively and affectionately approach them, similar to how they act when you get home from work.

Another misconception is that some breeds are automatically ideal with children. If you assume that your dog is going to be friendly with your child because of which breed he is, you may be in for an unfortunate surprise. Breed is not a reliable indicator of a dog's friendliness toward people. Please don't fall into this trap, or you could be putting your child and her human playmates at risk. Visualize two breeds of dog known for being good with children and friendly towards everyone. I can easily name first-hand, real-life examples of individuals of those breeds seriously threatening children. Breed A became extremely predatory toward the baby the day she was brought home from the hospital. Breed B knocked down the four-year-old son of the family, and dragged him across the yard by the arm.

Dogs certainly have behavior and temperament traits that are particular to their breed. After all, selecting for certain predictable behaviors is one of the motivations humans have had for creating breeds in the first place. But regardless of what the breed stereotype tells you about predicting your dog's behavior, it is foolhardy to ignore the behavior of your individual dog. Now is the time to step back and make a list of things your dog has done in the past, whether it was yesterday or more than a year ago, and evaluate whether or not your dog may need some behavior modification before the baby comes home. See the behavior check list at the end of this chapter for more information. When in doubt, seek out professional assistance as far in advance of the baby's arrival as possible.

Review Disease Prevention with Your Veterinarian and Doctor

Ask your veterinarian about this. She or he can talk with you about which kinds of parasites or bacteria can affect your child and how to prevent transmission. Make an appointment well in advance so you can rid your dog of fleas and ticks and decide on a prevention plan. Keep your yard clean of all dog feces. Your vet will likely want to make sure your dog is taking hookworm and roundworm preventative. With these preventative measures in place, there is no need to give up your dog in order to keep your child free of dog diseases. Parasite prevention and routine hygiene, like hand washing, keep most children safe.

Plan for How You Will Prevent Jealousy

Your baby's arrival will mean budgeting your time differently than you did before. That's true for everything, not just "dog time." By planning ahead, you and your dog can put new routines in place so that they are familiar habits by the time the baby arrives. If you start new routines as soon as possible (preferably no later than four weeks before the baby's due date), it will make a big difference for everyone's stress level. A dog trainer can be a big help here and can recommend creative, time-efficient ways to exercise your dog's mind and body according to her individual needs. Meet your dog's daily needs for affection, exercise, and mental stimulation, and she will likely adjust to the new schedule very well. Here are a few easy but highly effective ways to meet your dog's needs:

- Enlist the help of a neighbor or relative to walk or play fetch with your dog, or use a well-run doggie daycare during especially hectic times.

- Have your dog sit before any interaction with her (petting, putting the leash on, offering water, everything). This is like mental gymnastics, which will exercise her mind while instilling good habits.

- Substitute the boring dog food bowl for some serious fun. Feed your dog in the safety zone (explained in the next section) by using a kibble-dispensing food puzzle like those available through Busy Buddy toys. She'll love it!

· See the section in chapter 1 on how to create for your dog a
positive association with your baby.

Identify Behaviors That Need
Professional Attention Before the Baby Arrives

If you think your dog may have a problem with aggression, shyness, or aloofness with people, consult with a qualified dog behavior expert. Your veterinarian can provide a referral to a veterinary behaviorist or other qualified behavior consultant. If you are uneasy about the way your dog acts around children, adults, other dogs, other animals, or new things in general, then now is the time to investigate this with a professional. Don't wait.

Past behavior is an excellent predictor of future behavior. But be aware that aggression in one situation may or may not be related to aggression in another. A qualified behavior consultant can meet you and your dog, take a thorough history, observe your dog's behavior, assess the risks for you, and discuss with you the chances of resolving the behavior issue. It may well be that your dog would be best off in another home and that your child would be best off if your dog had a new home. Just don't jump into such a big step without exploring all the options. If you need to find a new home for your dog, that will be a difficult decision and one with which you'll be glad you had professional help.

If your dog has displayed any of the behaviors or characteristics listed below, it is best to address them professionally right away, before the baby comes and you are too tired and busy to take on a new project. Some behavior modification protocols can be very successful, but they take weeks and months to yield the results you'll need. Some are simply too risky to undertake with a child in the home. Get qualified assistance as soon as possible, so you'll have plenty of time to sort everything out before your baby's arrival. It may turn out that you will need just a few suggestions to help your dog. Think of it as an important part of baby preparation for your dog.

Suppose both parents don't agree that the dog may have a problem. In my experience with couples who are expecting a child, usually one member of the couple thinks the dog may have an issue, while the other person denies it. The parent in denial may make excuses for why the dog behaved that way "only the one time" or "only with certain people" or just because he was "being protective." Please remember that your child's safety is at stake, so this is no time to put a spin on things. Part of your job as a responsible dog owner and a sensible parent is to get your dog the help he needs, not to downplay things that could be a red flag. It doesn't mean that you have a bad dog, it means you are looking out for your dog and everyone involved. You have nothing to lose if you seek help that your dog doesn't urgently need, but a lot to lose if he needs help and doesn't get it.

Many dogs will have done at least one thing on the following list. Only a qualified professional can help determine how serious or risky the behavior is, and how big a threat it may pose to your child or others. The point is to avoid falling into the trap most people fall into. They don't recognize the behaviors below as signs of potential trouble, then they are surprised and devastated if there is a bite. You can avoid all that by taking an inventory of your dog's past behavior, comparing it to this list, and heading off a potentially risky situation by getting help now.

Some of the following behaviors are not necessarily a direct threat to your child, but will at the minimum make living with the dog and baby more challenging than is necessary. For example, if your dog reacts aggressively toward other dogs on leash walks, it may pose an indirect threat to your baby, since it could make walking with the dog and the stroller very dangerous. Other issues pose more of a direct risk to the baby, like a dog who is tense about being approached when she's resting or has something of value in her possession, like a dog toy that may interest your child. Remember that your baby will soon be moving about, exploring, and attempting to interact with your dog. Your child's playmates and their parents will soon be coming over to visit. Let a qualified professional assess your dog and help you plan for success while you still have the luxury of time to address these issues.

Obtain a referral from your veterinarian and get started now if your dog:

- barks or lunges at dogs on walks

- barrels past you down the stairs or out the door

- is shy or easily startled

- is noise sensitive (cowering or cringing in fear, or barking frantically)

- gets anxious about certain situations like thunderstorms or being left alone

- is aggressive toward another dog, at home or away from home, on leash or off

- is wary of people, or is okay with some people but not others

- is sensitive about having her space invaded by people or dogs

- uses her mouth, struggles, or growls when touched certain places

- gets grouchy over touch or handling, like grooming or having paws wiped off

- gets tense when people approach if he has a toy, food, or is on a resting place

- guards possessions or food when someone tries to take them away

- barks and cannot calm down if she sees someone outside the house or when the doorbell rings (possibly exhibiting threatening body language like tail held high or hackles up)

- barks (and cannot calm down) at strangers on the street or visitors to your home

- seems fearful of adults or kids of any age

- is easily fired up, either in play or other reason, and has a hard time calming down

- uses her mouth on your body or gets out of control during play or greeting

- uses her body to cut you off from hugging or touching a person or other dog

- barks at, lunges at, or chases kids, joggers, cyclists, or skateboarders

- avoids, ignores, or is disinterested in children or adults

- is generally aloof with people

- has growled at, snapped at, nipped, or bitten a child or adult

- exhibited any other behavior that concerns you, even a little.

If you can't quite put your finger on it, but you've felt afraid of your dog at times, or your dog seems out of control sometimes, please get professional assistance. It's better to be safe than sorry.

The Safety Zone

What is the safety zone?

Imagine some typical household scenarios once you have a child: perhaps you are throwing a birthday party or hosting a play date, or maybe your toddler is just feeling extra energetic and zooming around the house. Wouldn't it be great if your dog had somewhere to get away from all this activity, to take a break from all that potentially stressful stimulation? Or suppose you don't have time to monitor your child and dog as carefully as you'd like or you'd rather sit and play a new game with your child. Wouldn't it be great if you and your child could take a break from the dog? While your dog may currently have the run of the house, the furniture, and your attention, in the not-too-distant future there will be times when you wish you could ask him to lie down quietly in his own designated spot. Your dog needs a spot that will allow him to relax, undisturbed by children, and this will mean greater safety for your child and his playmates.

That spot is called the safety zone. It is an indoor, child-free zone where your dog can be temporarily confined. This section will teach you how to set up the safety zone so your dog will love it. The safety zone is an important tool for helping to ensure the well-being of your child and your dog, not to mention your sanity.

Make the safety zone an inviting retreat for your dog. This exercise pen has a closable door built into one of the panels, making entry and exit more convenient.
Photo by author.

Where should the safety zone be?

The safety zone could be a room, or an area within a room, that is near household activities but does not require you to move in and out of it frequently. Choose a room in which you can confine your dog such that he can still smell, hear, and even partly see many household activities, without being in the thick of things. For some people, the dining room works well. Here are some options:

1. If you can spare a whole room, a baby gate is a fine option. They are made now in a wide variety of heights and widths. Buy an appropriate height so your dog cannot climb or leap over the gate. In catalogues they always show the babies and dogs on the same side of the gate. That's just for marketing, of course. In real life, your dog will not be disturbed within the safety zone and your child will never be in the safety zone with your dog.

2. If your dog is crate-trained, this is a good time to reintroduce that tool. Make sure the crate is large enough for the dog to stand, turn around, and lie down in comfortably. If your dog is already house-trained, you may consider purchasing a larger crate than the one you have, for extra space and comfort for your pooch. The crate should be kept in a room near the main living areas of the house. One benefit of the crate is that it is portable, so that your dog can sleep in it at night, either near you or on the same level of the house.

3. Another portable safety zone is something called an exercise pen, which is similar in concept to a child's playpen. You may see it referred to as an x-pen for short. It's like a crate without a floor or a roof, made of wire panels that you can collapse, fold up, and carry or store. They also come in a variety of sizes and heights. I recommend the type with a door that latches for easy entry and exit by your dog.

4. If necessary, it is okay to use more than one safety zone so that you have an alternative spot in another part of the house. You can also alternate safety zones and their locations so your dog does not become overly attached to any one spot. If you do this, just be sure it is clear to your child that it is still the dog's special zone. When in doubt, designate only one safety zone.

When to introduce the safety zone

Introduce the safety zone as soon as possible, but preferably no later than four weeks before the baby's arrival. This will give you ample time to teach your dog to enjoy the safety zone and to recognize a verbal cue to go there when you ask her to. The sooner you make the safety zone part of your dog's normal routine, the sooner she will enjoy it and take it in stride as no big deal, which is just the attitude you will want her to have once the baby arrives. If your dog is especially clingy or needy, or has been distressed by confinement or separation from you in the past, start introducing the safety zone as soon as possible. If you are concerned about this, enlist the help of a dog trainer or behavior consultant who can help you find the quickest path to success. It sure beats making the problem worse by using trial and error or picking a strategy that takes too long to work. This is no time to wing it.

Multi-dog households

If you have more than one dog of about equal size, and they have never squabbled over space, food, or toys, then one safety zone for both dogs can work. Just make sure the room you choose is large enough. Monitor them closely at first. However, if you've chosen crates or x-pens, each dog will need their own safety zone.

How to teach your dog to love the safety zone

You will be spending less time with your dog after the baby arrives. This is perfectly okay. There's no need to feel guilty if you prepare your dog properly. Besides, by introducing the safety zone before baby's arrival, you'll help your dog think of the safety zone as a welcome rest, not as a sign that the baby is hogging your attention. If the safety zone is the source of happy experiences for your dog, she will likely feel happy there. The idea is to teach your dog to look forward to spending time there, away from you.

Here's how to introduce the safety zone:

1. Feed your dog all her meals in the safety zone. Use hollow, food dispensing toys (food puzzles) such as Kong or Busy Buddy brands, or a hollowed-out juice jug with holes cut into it. Leave the access door to the safety zone open. If it turns out your dog is inclined to take the food puzzle out of the safety zone to eat her meal, then tie the toy to a chair leg or to the back of the crate. Keep the door open for the first few meals. After a couple of days, feed your dog all her meals with the door closed.

2. Between meals, when your dog is not watching, sprinkle some outrageously good treats in the safety zone. Let her find them on her own. She'll think, "Well, I'll be! The safety zone sprouts special goodies!"

3. After a day or two, introduce short periods with the door closed. With your pooch chewing her special edible toy in the safety zone, go take a shower, pay the bills, or check the mail. Start with five-minute activities, then gradually increase the time each time you practice. Once you work up to fifteen- to thirty-minute activites (like preparing dinner or watching a TV show), occasionally and nonchalantly toss a yummy treat to your dog. If your dog has been anxious about separation from you in the past, start by sitting a in a chair near the safety zone. Read a book or write thank-you notes. At each meal, gradually move the chair further from the safety zone until you are out of sight.

Creature comforts

Provide fresh water and comfy bedding for your dog in the safety zone.

In order to prevent your dog from barking or whining while in the safety zone, try some of the approaches listed below:

- Always provide safe, edible chew toys in the safety zone, such as Nylabones.

- Provide your puppy or dog with plenty of aerobic exercise. A tired dog is a good dog.

- Choose a spot for the safety zone near family activities and near your sleeping area at night. Dogs are social creatures and should not be isolated.

- If you're using a crate, you can cover most of it with a light sheet or towel, but be sure not to block air circulation.

- Ignore whining or it will escalate. A much more effective strategy is to prevent it to begin with by following the above plan closely.

How to get your dog to go into the safety zone on cue

Stand about two feet from the safety zone with your dog. Hold your dog by the collar or gently push back on her chest to keep her from moving toward the safety zone. This is a little bit of reverse psychology, plus she will be inclined to push forward against something pushing on her. Continue holding her by the collar and let her see you toss a tidbit into the crate. Pause so she strains forward a bit, thinking, "I really want to go in there!" Then release the collar and let her go. As she surges toward the safety zone, give a verbal cue like "nap time!" or "kennel!" It doesn't matter what verbal cue you use, just be consistent and say it only once. She will hop into the safety zone and get the treat. Practice this five or six times in quick succession. Feed her meals like this for a couple of days, a handful of food at a time, and she'll soon have the idea.

If your dog doesn't seem very motivated to zip right in, or he isn't particularly wild about food, try any combination of these three approaches:

1. Make sure you're feeding him on a strict schedule and not "free feeding." Food won't be all that motivating for him if it sits out in his bowl all the time.

2. Let him watch you put something delicious in the safety zone, but *don't* let him go in after it. Shut the crate door or the baby gate with the yummy thing on the inside, and the dog on the outside. He'll soon feel quite motivated to get in the safety zone. Say the verbal cue "nap time!" then open the door and he will hop in. Don't lock him in yet; just let him enjoy what he found inside.

3. Make entering the safety zone into a game. (What dog can resist a good game?) A few times a day, position your dog near the safety zone. Say "nap time!" or "kennel!" He'll enter the safety zone, and you'll surprise him by not shutting the door. Instead, say "okay!" and encourage him to come right back out again. The game is that sometimes the reward for going into the safety zone on cue is being briefly confined with a treat, but sometimes the reward is that as soon as your dog enters the safety zone, you say, "okay!" and let him come right back out. This will help the dog associate the safety zone with fun and surprising rewards.

When to use the safety zone

Use the safety zone any time you cannot actively coach your dog and child through their interactions (more on this in the section on being a kid canine coach in chapter 3). As long as you continue to meet your dog's daily needs for aerobic exercise, affection, and training, there is no need to feel guilty about using the safety zone. Trust me, your dog will thank you for giving him some peace and quiet. Using the safety zone may well prevent your child from rushing up to your dog, startling him, or hurting him unintentionally. You may also find it useful when company comes over, when your child's playmates are visiting, when you're not home, whenever you have a babysitter or housekeeper over, or any time front-door traffic might pose an opportunity for doggie escape.

If introduced early and used properly, the safety zone can be a big plus for everyone in the family. It is designed to keep stress levels low by providing breaks for everyone, and to confine the dog when you cannot actively coach his interactions with your child. It is a practical, humane, effective way to prevent injury and stress.

Creatures of Habit

Most people would agree that their dog is a creature of habit. Habits and daily routines help dogs feel more secure. For your dog, engaging in certain expected rituals with you gives some order to the universe. Your dog really has very little control over his daily life and is very dependent on you to meet his needs and regulate his activities. This is true even before your baby joins the family! After the baby arrives, the so-called routine may change on a daily, if not hourly, basis.

The good news is that you can start some routines in advance that will help smooth the transition for your baby's arrival. These routines will help offer a sense of security and well-being to your dog, even when things get a little hectic or unpredictable after your baby comes home. However, these routines should be introduced gradually and used consistently. Trying to change these routines as you go, or changing them all at once when the baby arrives, could be too stressful for your dog and for you. There is no need to add to your stress level once you are caring for a baby, nor to have the baby's arrival signal more stress from your dog's perspective.

First and foremost, it is important to meet your dog's daily needs for exercise and mental stimulation. Make sure he gets enough aerobic exercise. Hanging out in the yard, even if

To get her dog in the habit of lying calmly at their feet before the new baby arrives, this mother feeds a treat or two to make calm behavior rewarding for her dog.
Photo by author.

he occasionally chases a squirrel or roughhouses with a dog buddy, is not adequate. He must enjoy sustained aerobic activity a couple of times a day (usually fifteen to twenty minutes each). Start providing this yourself or trade chores with a neighbor who will do it for you. You may have to hire a dog walker or doggie day care to help you. If you use a dog walker and/or day care, start well in advance, at least occasionally, so it will be familiar to all involved before the baby's arrival.

To exercise your dog's mind and instill good manners, start using the doggie version of "say please." Your dog should sit before he receives access to anything that he likes. Each interaction should be a little puzzle for him to figure out. By doing this he will have control over what happens to him next, because he will be thinking, "I can get her to put my leash on by sitting quietly." As a nice bonus, you will have a more well-behaved dog. Anything meaningful that happens to your dog (like meals, leash walks, petting, or outdoor access) should be preceded by him sitting. His new motto will become, "When in doubt, sit." If you have a small dog, think of this as a doggie curtsey that asks, "Mother, may I?" For a thorough explanation of this new routine, please see the training section later in this chapter.

Begin using the safety zone when you are at home, as well as when you are away. This will teach your dog to enjoy relaxing on her own, even if you are in the next room. Make this no big deal, and your dog will accept time in the safety zone as relaxing quiet time. Once the baby arrives, your dog will not think of it as punishment, isolation, or withdrawal of your affection. It will just be relaxation time in the safety zone. As a nice bonus, there will be no fuss and no guilt for you at times when you really need to focus on the baby.

Begin feeding your dog's meals in the safety zone. Use fun and interesting food puzzles to provide the mental stimulation your dog needs. I recommend sturdy, hollow toys such as Tricky Treats Puzzle Ball, Twist-n-Treat, Kong, Roll-a-Treat, or Squirrel Dude. Rotate the toys every few days to keep things interesting. The nice bonus here is that your dog will learn to love her safety zone, will learn to be quiet there, and will have her mental needs met in a way that is easy for you.

There are about to be a lot of changes and a lot of new emotions in the house. To help keep your dog as emotionally even-keeled as possible, it's important to do something for her that might not be easy for you: begin consistently practicing nonchalant greetings and departures. This is difficult for most dog owners until they see it from their dog's perspective. Please don't put your dog on an emotional rollercoaster, hyped up when you return, only to dread when you go, wringing her paws while you're away and getting hysterical when you return. This can happen if you make a fuss over her when you leave and have a huge celebration when you return. Be nonchalant. Your dog has no control over when you go and when you return. If you make a production out of these comings and goings, which should be normal, uneventful parts of your dog's day, you are not being fair to your dog. Petting your dog, feeding treats, reminding her to be a good girl, and saying things like "Don't forget, mommy loves you, snookums!" on your way out the door could help turn your dog into an emotional basket case. Don't pay much attention to your dog five or ten minutes before you leave, and when you return home pay your dog little attention for five or ten minutes before greeting him. If you feel you must speak to your dog, say something nonchalant such as "Have a nice nap, see you later," or "Hey, how was your nap?" as you check through the mail or change your clothes. It is very flattering when our dogs go gaga over us, but it's not a very nice thing to do to them over and over.

Make a plan for where you want your dog to be when you are engaged in new routines with your baby. While you won't be able to predict perfectly what will happen or when, you can make a list of likely baby-related activities such as:

- nursing

- napping

- playing on the floor

- walking with the stroller

- entertaining visitors who've come to see the baby

- changing a diaper

- sitting on the couch holding the baby

- pacing back and forth with the baby

- sleeping at night

- riding in the car

- spending time in the nursery.

To prepare your dog for the new routines all you have to do is follow the these steps:

1. Ask yourself, "Where will the dog be while the baby is _____ (fill in the blank)?"

2. Practice all of these situations with your dog and a lifelike baby doll.

3. Pair the activity with calm praise and treats for your dog.

For example, there may be times you will need the option of having your baby in the bed with you at night. Ask yourself now, "Where will the dog be while the baby's being nursed in the bed?" A good answer would be "on his dog bed in our room." You will then start having your dog sleep on his dog bed in your room instead of up on the bed with you. Start doing that as soon as possible, so it won't be a difficult thing for you or for him once the baby has arrived.

Here are some other suggestions for where the dog should be during typical baby activities. These may be new routines for your dog, so start them well in advance:

- Car rides: Use a crate or doggie seatbelt. Occupy your dog with a chew toy that he is crazy about. Cover the crate with a light sheet if he is excitable in the car. If you use a doggie seatbelt, accustom him to the harness around the house for a few days before going on a ride (let him wear it while he's eating a meal). Start with short rides to fun places.

- Walking with the stroller: Use a doll and accustom your dog to walking politely alongside the stroller. Do not wrap the leash around your hand or around the stroller handle. Both of these could cause serious injury to you or your baby. Instead, teach your dog leash manners. If your dog pulls like a maniac or is fond of lunging out at things unexpectedly, get the help of a dog trainer right off the bat. This will save you time and stress, as proper leash walking can take a few weeks to instill.

- Sitting on the couch: Whether you're nursing or just hanging out with your baby, your dog should not be up on the couch with you. However, your dog should not be totally excluded either. Reward your dog for lying at your feet or somewhere nearby, or enlist the help of a dog trainer to teach him to go to a nearby mat on cue. Practice holding a doll and cooing to it so that your dog will learn to remain lying down even if he hears excited sounds. If you have a dog who has a calm personality, you could teach him to do a down-stay beside you on the couch. Teach him to hop up only with permission (after he's done a sit, of course; more on this in the section later in chapter 1 on "The Top Three Cues Your Dog Should Respond to and How to Teach Them").

Rehearse leash walks with the stroller before the baby arrives.
Photo Courtesy of Stephanie Weatherly.

- Playing on the floor: Your dog should be in the safety zone. Teach him to relax there while you coo at and play with a doll baby. Reward your dog with treats or a food puzzle.

- Spending time in the nursery: Dogs who tend to be aloof, rowdy, or out of control should be taught to stay out of the nursery. Use the safety zone, or use a baby gate or screen door at the nursery threshold and reward the dog when she lies quietly outside the room. If your dog is generally calm and very people-oriented, then it is a matter of personal preference as to whether you allow the dog into the nursery. Either way, start practicing before the baby arrives. If you'd like the dog to learn to come in, just spend quiet, low-key time in the nursery with your dog. Hold a baby doll, pretend to change a diaper, sing to the doll, coo to it in the crib or bassinet, pace around with it, and sit and rock it. Pick an activity or two to practice about once a day. Reward your dog with treats for relaxing nearby, and tell her what a good girl she is.

Reward your dog for lying quietly beside the couch while you hold a baby doll.
Photo by author.

· Nap time: This will be time to cherish, and you certainly
won't want the dog interrupting it. If your dog tends to
patrol the windows for squirrels or passersby, barking when
they come into view, by all means keep him in his safety
zone or enclosed in an area of the house with you during
your baby's nap time. You might also wish to brush or
massage your dog at this time, which could be a calming
activity for both of you. If your dog is likely to bark
because it's the time of day when the letter carrier arrives
or you're expecting a visitor, consider occupying your dog
with a complex food puzzle in your fenced-in back yard
(provided he cannot bark at people from the yard). If you
choose this option, check on your dog frequently to make
sure he's not bored or agitated. Those are states of mind
that can lead to barking. Remember not to pay attention
to your dog only while your baby is napping, or he'll
quickly associate getting attention and feeling happy with
your baby's absence.

· Departures and Arrivals: Keep them calm and polite. "See you later," is about all you should say when you leave. When you return, ignore your dog for about five minutes. Check through your mail, change your shoes, rummage in the fridge to see what's for dinner. When your dog is perfectly calm, then greet him. He should sit first, of course, which should be a piece of cake if you've been practicing doggie "say please." While he sits, greet him calmly and gently. Reward him with treats for working on learning this new skill. If he gets up, stand tall and look away, as though you suddenly turned into a tree. Respond to your dog only when he sits again. Make sure to keep the interaction short and low-key to help your dog succeed. This skill will keep your baby much safer. It will prevent a big dog from leaping and inadvertently scratching the baby or making you lose your balance. It will prevent a small dog from making a commotion or getting dangerously underfoot. Teach your dog that your coming and going is a time of calm, and reward his calm sitting with calm attention from you.

Nap time is quiet time

If your dog makes a lot of noise with his I.D. tags, consider putting them in a tiny Velcro pouch that attaches to the collar. The pouch is called Quiet Spot and is available on-line.

Pre-baby Veterinary Check-up

Before your baby arrives, it's wise to make sure your dog is feeling his best and that he knows how to mind his manners. The next two sections will show you what to do to get your dog the veterinary and training tune-ups he needs. You'll be glad you planned ahead for successful child-dog interactions.

Dogs can be stoic creatures. It's sometimes hard to tell that your dog is uncomfortable or even in pain, but it's important to make sure your dog is feeling well. Think about it this way: how tolerant do you feel toward someone, even someone you like, when you have a headache or a backache?

Take your dog in for a thorough veterinary exam. Do this even if your dog has already had his annual exam and vaccinations. Tell your veterinarian you are expecting a baby and that you want to make sure your dog is free of pain, discomfort, and parasites.

Work with your vet to address any potential health issues before the baby arrives. Here are some questions to ask your vet, even if she doesn't bring them up.

Does my dog have pain or discomfort anywhere?

Your vet will likely ask you questions about your dog's daily activities, examine and touch him all over, take his temperature, obtain a stool sample, and possibly take a blood sample or x-rays. It is better to be thorough than to risk your dog feeling physically uncomfortable around your child. Dogs who are uncomfortable or in pain can be grumpy. If your dog is feeling cranky and is approached or annoyed by your child, he may be more likely to react by biting.

Waistline-friendly dog training

Training your dog with treats does not mean that he must gain weight. Use your dog's meal time as training time, using the kibble pieces in place of treats. Or you can use delicious low-calorie treats like macaroni noodles cooked in broth instead of water. Ask your vet about other low-calorie foods to use as rewards for your dog.

Is my dog overweight?

From what I have seen over the years, most family dogs are overweight. Overweight dogs have a harder time staying cool and comfortable, particularly once the temperature reaches about 60 degrees. Their bodies, including their joints, are also under greater stress. Even if your dog is just a few pounds overweight, this might represent a huge percentage of his body weight. When you consider that your dog will soon be eating extra tidbits that the new baby will be "feeding" from the high chair, it's important to start your dog at an ideal weight.

How much and what type of exercise should my dog get each day?

You will probably find that you need to increase the amount of exercise your dog gets, to help with both weight loss and putting your dog on his best behavior. Your vet can make suggestions as to what sort of exercise is right for your dog, taking into account his individual history, age, and breed. Adequate aerobic exercise is an important way to spend quality time with your dog each day. Giving your dog attention in this way can also help prevent unwanted attention-seeking behaviors.

How are my dog's hearing and vision?

This is especially important for older dogs. You will want to know about this so you can help your dog cope with hearing and vision loss, learn to communicate with your dog in new ways (using hand signals, for example) before the baby's arrival, and help your child avoid unintentionally surprising your dog.

Does my dog have allergies?

Imagine if your skin felt itchy much of the time. How would you like being touched? What kind of mood would you be in? Other areas of the body can be affected by allergies such as the digestive system, ears, or anal glands, which can contribute to your dog's discomfort.

Is my dog free of internal and external parasites?

Roundworms and hookworms, as well as fleas and ticks, can be transmitted from dog to person and can be harmful to children. Make sure your dog is free of these parasites and that you have an active prevention strategy in place.

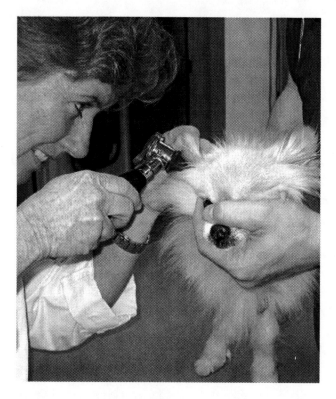

Have your vet perform a thorough exam before your baby arrives.
Photo by author.

My dog has exhibited behavior that concerns me. Can you recommend a trainer or behavior consultant in the area?

Your vet is a good source of referrals and should be prepared to provide you with the names and contact information of qualified, professional dog experts in your area. The appendix of this book also includes directories of qualified trainers who use modern methods.

The Three Secrets to a Well-Behaved Dog

Before the baby comes, after the baby arrives, and throughout junior's childhood, continue to meet your dog's daily needs, prevent behavior you don't like, and reward good behavior. The amount of energy, frustration, and trouble these steps will save you can hardly be overstated:

1. Meet Your Dog's Daily Needs

Aerobic Exercise
Benefits: helps prevent destructive chewing, nuisance barking, jumping up, and other forms of attention-seeking behavior. A tired dog is a good dog.

How to: Most adolescent dogs need twenty to thirty minutes exercise at least two or three times a day. Try playing fetch, hiking, swimming, jogging, brisk walking, and find-it games. Get approval for jogging or brisk walking from your vet first. Hire a dog walker, trade chores with a neighbor for walking your dog, or consider doggie day care.

Diet and Correct Feeding Routine
Benefits: speeds house-training, helps prevent destructive chewing, pushy behavior, and vocalizing in the safety zone.

How to: Feed high-quality food on a regular schedule. Do not "free feed." Allow your dog fifteen minutes per meal and remove any leftovers. Always provide fresh water. Feed meals with food puzzles like stuffed Kong or Busy Buddy toys.

The Right Kind of Attention
Benefits: helps prevent dog from engaging in attention-seeking mischief. The health benefits for many people include reduced stress and heart rate.

How to: Dogs are highly social creatures, which is part of why we enjoy living with them. Spend time each day exercising, training, and grooming your dog. All attention should begin with doggie "say please" (see below.) If your dog demands attention by pawing, nudging, barking, or shoving a toy at you, respond by looking away, and leave the room if she persists. Be consistent. Dogs will do what is effective to gain your attention, so make the standard calm, polite sitting.

2. Prevent behavior you don't like

If you don't want your dog jumping up, counter-surfing, running away, getting up on the furniture, whining in his confinement area, or getting into the trash or laundry basket, you must prevent these. Punishing your dog after the fact will do little good and could even make matters worse by creating unintended fallout, including aggression. Prevention is the key. The following are some tricks of the trade to help you prevent unwanted behavior:

- · When you're home, tether your dog to a piece of furniture and always provide an edible chew toy.

- · Use a safety zone like a crate or baby-gated room (always providing edible chew toys and fresh water).

- · Use a baby gate to keep your dog from areas that are off limits (such as a cat room or the kitchen during meal preparation).

- · Leash your dog outdoors to prevent running away. Leash your dog indoors to prevent jumping on guests.

- · Under supervision, let your dog drag a lightweight leash indoors. Step on it to gain instant control or to prevent undesirable behavior like jumping up, counter-surfing, or climbing up on furniture.

- · Use a dog pacifier. Good choices are brands such as Kong, Roll-a-Treat, Groove Thing, Nylabone Edibles, and Greenies. Meals can be fed with Kong, Roll-a-Treat, or Busy Buddy. Kong and Groove Thing can be stuffed with kibble and a bit of peanut butter. Stuffed Kongs can be microwaved or frozen. Keep your dog busy before she gets bored and finds her own way to amuse herself.

- · Dogproof your house, or at least a room or two, by removing all valuable or dangerous items that are less than three feet off the ground.

3. Reward behavior you do like

Once you've prevented the behavior you don't like, you can teach and reward behavior you do like, such as coming when called and following commands like leave it, sit/stay, and go to your safety zone. Doggie "say please" is a great starting point. It's a voluntary "sit" and should precede access to anything your dog values.

Benefits: your dog learns self-control, practices "sit" so much it becomes the default behavior, and learns to pay better attention to you. The "say please" automatic sit prevents undesirable behavior like jumping up, sniffing crotches, plowing through doorways, demanding food, and getting wound up when visitors arrive.

How to: Wait for your dog to sit before giving her anything of value (you may cue her with her cue to "sit" for the first few days to help give her the idea). This is the doggie version of saying please. After she sits, give an "okay" to release her to eat meals, go through the front door, get affection, meet a new friend, get fresh water, have the leash put on, start a game of fetch, hop into or out of the car, greet family members, and absolutely everything else your dog likes. Ask yourself, "Is this something my dog would like?" If so, she should first say please by doing a sit. Then say, "okay" to give her what she wants. What a polite, responsive pooch you'll have!

The Top Three Cues Your Dog Should Respond to and How to Teach Them

You may have already taught your dog some basic cues like sit and lie down. If so, this would be a good time to polish up on them. Polished means you've taught your dog well enough so that she complies the first time you give a cue, even under distraction, and without you bribing her with a treat. You may consider enrolling in a group class where the focus is doggie basic manners around the house. Or you may benefit from having a professional training session or two in your home. (See the appendix for books and videos to help you or visit www.apdt.com for a dog trainer near you.)

If you are ready to dive in on your own and polish up what you've taught her in the past, then this section is for you. It covers three main skills at which your dog should be proficient in preparation for your baby's arrival. Don't have a lot of time? Not to worry, the most important skill of all is the easiest to teach. This first skill is the dog version of "saying please," which is all about teaching your dog to spontaneously exhibit calm, polite behavior. The second skill to polish up is your dog's "come" cue. Finally, to help prevent stress and injury, you will learn the "nose touch," a nifty strategy for quickly moving your dog out of dicey child-dog situations.

Bear in mind that these training suggestions are for dogs who are free of existing behavioral problems. They will not cure a dog of serious, problematic behavioral tendencies. Consult the appendix and contact a qualified expert if your dog exhibits any of the behaviors listed in the "Can you keep your dog?" section at the beginning of this chapter.

No more pulling on leash

Is your dog a pain in the neck to walk on the leash? If so, you may need the help of a professional dog trainer. If your dog is in the habit of pulling you around or lunging out at distractions, it can take weeks to change her behavior. In the meantime, try an Easy Walk harness. This particular brand seems to yield success with most dogs because, unlike a traditional harness, the leash attachment is located on a special loop at the dog's chest. It doesn't hurt the dog and cuts down on pulling dramatically.

Happy Kids, Happy Dogs

A note on methodology

Regardless of how you may have trained your dog up until now, I strongly recommend using modern, gentle, dog-friendly methods from now on. Applying modern dog-training methods means never having to yell at your dog, smack him, knee him, spray him, jerk his collar, or cause pain or distress in any way. Although some of these older methods do give the results that people want, the unintended side effects are simply not worth it, especially with children around. Since these methods make dogs feel threatened, dogs who are trained using these methods can become suspicious and even fearful of humans, causing them to become more easily startled or stressed and more likely to use aggression to defend themselves or avoid people altogether. I doubt you want your dog feeling like this with your child around.

Dogs are incredibly flexible, and most dogs readily welcome modern, reward-based training methods. Because this thoughtful, gentle training is so effective, there's really no reason to use the harsher approaches that create unintended fallout. As explained in the introduction, we will be using food and other types of rewards. You won't believe how much fun it is for you and for your dog to get fast, excellent results.

Teaching your dog how to say "please"

The goal: The most important training tune-up for your dog before your baby arrives is to teach her the doggie equivalent of saying please. This means she will learn to sit, automatically (without being told), before she gets anything, even if she is very excited. This will instill in your dog's mind the following rule: "When in doubt, sit."

The benefits: Having a dog who recognizes and performs doggie please is like the difference between having a teenager who says, "Gimme the car keys!" and one who says, "May I please borrow the car?" The second teenager is much easier to live with. If your dog is sitting politely, waiting for her next instruction, she can't possibly be jumping up, bolting through a door, yanking you down the steps, lunging toward visitors, leaping on or knocking over the baby.

How to teach: First you'll need to teach your dog how to sit on cue. (Skip this part if your dog already responds reliably to your "sit" cue at least 80 percent of the time in a variety of circumstances.) Then, you'll show your dog how to use the sit position to get everything that matters to him. Finally, you'll use some advanced techniques so that your dog will sit for a duration even when there are exciting things going on around him. It's easy and fun to teach.

The modern method of teaching "sit" on cue
The big picture plan is to:

- Show your dog what to do instead of forcing him.

- Reward your dog for the goal behavior by saying "yes" and feeding him treat.

- Teach your dog to remain sitting until you give him permission to get up.

- Use the treat only as a reward, not a bribe, to teach the hand signal.

- Add the verbal signal "sit" in the last step. This way it will be associated only with the polished goal behavior.

For best results, begin all training in a low-distraction environment. Use treats your dog is nuts about. Train for no more than five minutes at a time.

Step 1

- Lure your dog into a sit with a treat. This means he'll start out in a standing position. Hold a treat in your hand and let him lick at (but not eat) it as you very, very slowly (we are talking glacial speed) guide the treat back over his head toward the area between his ears. His nose will come up and his butt will go down into sit position.

- When his butt hits the ground, say "yes" to let him know that he has earned the treat by sitting.

- Feed him the treat and praise him quietly.

- Before he gets up of his own accord, give him permission by saying "okay" while looking away and moving away from him.

- Do this five or six times in a row.

- Then repeat the same process in all different parts of the house.

- Once your dog has gotten the hang of it in each room, try it outside, first in an easy location and then in harder ones.

Let the dog sniff and lick the treat as you very, very slowly draw it back between her ears.

Photos this page by author.

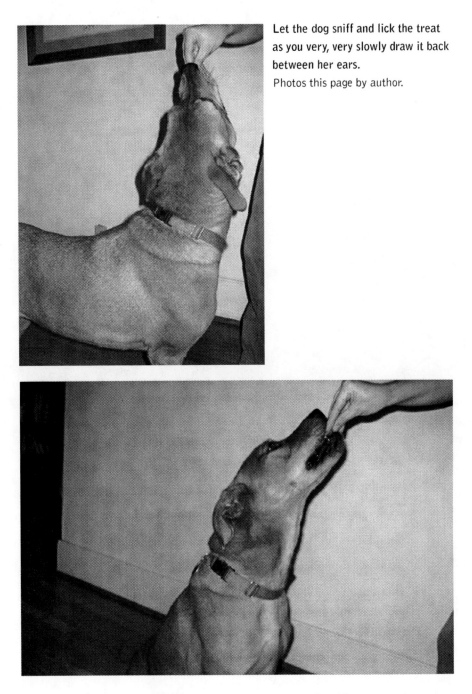

When the dog's rear end hits the floor in the sit position, say "yes!" to communicate that was the behavior that earns the treat, then feed the treat in the sit position.

Step 2

- Start over in the first room pretending to hold an invisible treat in the same hand in which you'd been holding the real treat. This will teach him the hand signal and eliminate the bribe.

- Repeat the same actions as in step 1, and when his butt hits the ground, say "yes" to let him know that he's earned the treat.

- Then feed him a treat from your other hand and praise him quietly.

- Before he gets up of his own accord, give him permission by saying "okay" while looking away and moving away from him.

- Repeat these same steps in each room of the house and in various locations outside.

Step 3

- Once you can use an invisible treat to get your dog to sit in any room and outside, you can start teaching him to respond to the verbal sit cue.

- Keep your hands at your sides. Without moving your hand say your dog's name, followed by, "Fido, sit."

- Pause for one second.

- Use the invisible treat to give your hand signal as usual.

- When he sits, say "yes" and feed him a treat.

- Say "okay" to give him permission to get up.

- After a few days of this, when he hears "Fido, sit," he will anticipate what comes next and begin sitting before you've even finished making your invisible treat hand signal.

- Once you've observed that, try offering the verbal cue, then just wait. He'll likely sit with no help from the hand cue.

- Say "yes" and feed him a few treats in a row, one at a time.

Troubleshooting: If he doesn't sit when you say it once, it means it is too hard for him. He is learning something new, so it is your job to help him succeed. Make it easier by eliminating distractions and using yummier treats, then try again.

Teaching your dog to "say please" without being asked
Identify everything your dog gets that he likes. This may include fresh water, meals, a treat, a nap on the furniture, a chance to come inside, a chance to go outside, the opportunity to hop into or out of the car, the chance to have the leash put on, a neck scratch, a butt scratch, having the leash taken off for free play, a game of fetch or tug, or the opportunity to play with another dog.

For the first few days, ask your dog to sit just before a favorite activity. Then, before you pet him, open the front door, or put the supper dish down, give your dog permission to get up by saying "okay." Then deliver what your dog was "saying please" for.

If you ask him to sit and he looks away or tries to wander off, calmly and quietly "body block" him by standing in front of him and moving toward him if necessary (but don't actually touch him with your body). Be silent and wait. Say each verbal cue only once. You can try staring at his rear end, which often yields immediate results. When he complies by sitting, respond instantly by saying "okay" and petting him, lowering the supper dish, opening the door, or doing whatever it was he earned by sitting so nicely. Since you want him to be fast at controlling himself and sitting, you need to be just as fast at rewarding. Here is an example with the correct sequence:

1. Dog looks expectant as you fill his food dish.

2. You cue him to sit with your verbal or hand cue.

3. Dog sits. (If he doesn't, silently body block or walk away.)

4. You say "okay."

5. You put his food dish down.

After a few days of saying "sit" and then saying "okay" before your dog gets something he likes, test your dog's understanding. Pick two of your dog's favorite things he has been doing a sit for (perhaps his supper and a chance to go outside), but this time do not actually say the word "sit." Believe it or not, your dog will remember the pattern and choose to sit all on his own in order to get what he wants. Do nothing. Just wait. Be absolutely silent. No hinting! It might take him thirty seconds or more, but he will sit, you will instantly say "okay," and then give him what he wants.

Left: Lisa simply waits for the dogs to sit, only then does she lower the bowls to the floor. As long as the dogs remain sitting, Lisa continues to lower the bowls. (Mattie, on the right, is actually in the "down" position, which is another good option if your dog knows that cue.) Right: Mico, on the left, gets excited and stands up, so Lisa instantly raises his bowl as a consequence. He sits again so quickly the camera can't catch him in the standing position. Photos by author.

After a couple of days of that silent waiting game, your dog will start sitting faster and faster for the things he really likes. This means it's time to try the same routine with things your dog likes, but isn't gaga over, like maybe his water when he is moderately thirsty. Just wait. He will start sitting automatically. Always release with "okay" before providing the goodie, so that he gets up with your permission and not just because he feels like it. So, the sequence becomes:

1. Dog looks expectant as you fill his water bowl.

2. You wait, standing there like a zombie holding the filled water dish.

Happy Kids, Happy Dogs

When Lisa is ready, she says "okay" to give permission for the dogs to stand up and eat. "Saying please" by sitting in exciting circumstances, like dinner time, teaches dogs self-control.
Photo by author.

3. Dog sits. (If he doesn't, continue to wait.)

4. You say "okay."

5. You put his water dish down.

Voila! You have taught him to say please by sitting for the things he values. This is especially helpful for dogs who could use a shot of confidence, as well as for dogs who seem to demand what they want with pushy behavior. Most dogs who use pushy behavior do so not because they're jerks, but because pushy behavior has been rewarded in the past. You can still turn over a new leaf, by rewarding calm, focused sitting. You have a choice. You can reward him for sitting calmly or you can inadvertently reward him for leaping up, barking, whining, and pawing at you. The behavior you choose to reward is the one you'll get more of.

Give the gift of self-control

Some people feel guilty about encouraging their dog to sit calmly in exchange for rewards. Let me hereby absolve you. You are giving your dog an incredibly humane and generous gift by providing this sense of structure and order to his universe. There is no punishment involved. Instead, the dog finally gets to use his wonderful brain, understands that life is orderly and safe, and learns to trust that you will hold up your part of the partnership by guiding him through what must seem like our kooky human world. Teach your dog to say please. You'll both be glad you did.

Advanced techniques for using say "please" to prepare for baby

- Instead of saying "yes" right away when your dog sits, count to two, then say "yes," feed him a treat, and then say "okay." Your dog has just done a two-second sit-stay—way to go! Over the next few days, work up to a ten-second sit. For best results, vary the number of seconds that elapse before you say "yes," rather than consistently increasing them. (Rewarding sit-stays of three-, one-, four-, three-, two-, and then six-second durations will make for a much stronger sit-stay than progressing in a linear fashion with durations one through six seconds).

- Cue your dog to sit. Without saying another word, put your hands on your head. Say "yes," and feed your dog a treat. Your dog has just held the sit position under mild distraction! Gradually work up to moving your arms and legs and speaking excitedly. Say "yes," and feed a treat when he sits for each distraction. Then get the kids (or grown-up helpers) in on the act. Play Simon Says so that you can keep everything under control and keep your dog successful. Always release your dog with "okay" when he has permission to get up.

- Practice getting him wound up (without kids present), and then ask him to sit. Say "yes" and feed a treat only for instantaneous sits.

- If your dog gets up before you give permission, just try again, but make it easier for him to succeed this time (i.e., with less talking or movement by you or the helper).

- Hold a baby doll in your arms or change the doll's diaper in the nursery. Reward your dog as usual for holding the sit position. Give permission to get up with "okay."

- Gradually build up to having your dog sit while you put the baby doll in the stroller in preparation for a walk. Have your dog sit while you sit on the couch with the baby doll, talking baby talk to the doll.

- Practice bringing the baby doll in the front door just like you will the day you bring your newborn baby home (see chapter 2 for details on this exercise).

After all of these exercises, your dog's default will begin to be: "The more I control myself and show patient and polite behavior, the quicker I get what I want. When in doubt, sit."

Teaching your dog to "come" when called

The goal: You say "Fifi, come!" and your dog instantly stops what she's doing, runs to you, and allows her collar to be held.

The benefits: It's much faster to call your dog away from an object or situation than it is to run over and intervene. Think pacifier that has dropped on the floor, think child who is about to have a meltdown, think diaper pail that has tipped over, think visiting child who is reaching to hug the dog. You get the picture.

Before getting started, there are some important principles to keep in mind.

- To dogs it must seem like a bizarre concept to stop doing something they find rewarding just to come over to us. Dogs do not understand human words until we carefully teach them, and they don't come into our lives knowing how to come when called. Be prepared to proceed slowly and build on success over time.

- If you are very generous with your rewards and *very carefully* add distractions like smells and dogs over the weeks and months, you will be on your way to being able to say, "My dog comes when called." It is a lot of work, a lot of fun, and well worth the effort.

- No matter how well trained your dog is, please obey leash laws and let your dog off leash only in safe, designated, fenced-in areas.

- If your dog has just encountered something fascinating, do not call her. During the learning phase, this is too challenging and she will fail. Calling your dog in situations where it is too difficult for her to comply will teach her to ignore you.

- Never scold your dog after she heeds a come command, even if she has just dug up your garden, chewed your shoe, or bolted out of the yard. You must prevent these to begin with by using a fence, a leash, a crate, and dog-proofed confinement areas like a baby-gated kitchen or safety zone.

- When she comes to you, do not ask your dog to sit. Reward her immediately for coming. Otherwise, she will soon think coming is no fun and avoid it. Do not scold her if she jumps up. To prevent her from jumping up, as your dog approaches you after being called, simply squat down before she reaches you, or hold your hands at knee level (she'll sniff them instead of jumping up).

- Never call your dog for something she considers unpleasant. If you need her near you to bring her inside, confine her, or give her a bath, go get her rather than calling her to come. Walk up to her, snap the leash on, and feed her a treat (in that order) so she'll think being caught is fabulous.

- If your dog sometimes does not respond to "come," switch to a different word and start over (Like "Fifi, here!") using the step-by-step instructions below.

How to teach your dog to come when called

Step 1: Responsiveness to her name

- Stand near her (about one foot away). Say "Fifi!" only once and in a happy voice.

- If she immediately makes eye contact, you should instantly acknowledge it with "yes" and feed her a treat.

- Increase your distance from her. Say her name cheerfully, once. When she makes eye contact, say "yes" and run the other way. Cheer excitedly as you run.

- When she catches up, feed her several pieces of food, one at a time. Feed her close to your body (to prevent her racing past you out of reach), with your hands low (to prevent jumping up).

- Practice the above steps three to five times a day. Sessions may range from one call to a few calls over a five minute period. Keep it short, fun, and successful.

Be picky. If your dog doesn't look up at you instantly when you call, you should instantly take off running away from her. As you run, remind her how much fun she's missing by babbling cheerful phrases like, "I've got your doggie biscuits! Oh my goodness, you've missed your chance!" She will undoubtedly follow you, and when she catches up offer her praise, but no treats. Make a mental note of why an attempt seemed too difficult for her to look up at you. On your next attempt, decrease the distance between you or the level of distraction accordingly. End each session on a successful note.

Repeat the steps above in the following locations in the order in which they are listed. Master each location before going on to the next:

- indoors, all rooms (using familiar rooms first, then less familiar ones)

- indoors with distraction, like a person walking by or animal noises on TV

- outdoors (using easy spots first and then more challenging areas)

- outdoors with mild distractions, like a toy lying still, then a toy moving

· outdoors with more challenging distractions, like a bird nearby or a person approaching.

Step 2: "Come" as a verbal cue

Do this only once you have completed all of step 1. Add the word "come" to your verbal cue, so that you'll now be saying, "Fifi, come!" while everything else stays the same. Practice "Fifi, come!" in each of the previous locations at a distance from you at which she can succeed. Always reward her success as in step 1. When you reward her, surprise her with dinner or other activities that she is crazy about, such as a car ride, a walk, or the chance to play with other dogs.

The following are some important tips:

· Controlling opportunities for using "come" successfully is the key, so avoid having her get loose accidentally. Outdoors keep her leashed or on a long line that you can use to reel her in (wear gloves if you use a long line, or step on it). Call only when you know she will succeed, otherwise go get her. Increase distance and distraction level gradually.

· Never call her for anything she perceives as unpleasant or even neutral (like having to come indoors). Otherwise, she will soon learn to tune you out.

· Reward generously and with variety: use different treats, play a raucous game of tug with her favorite toy, give her dinner that contains a few table scraps.

· For quicker results, feed her at least half her daily food intake as treats for coming.

Cheer your dog on

Most people don't cheer enough as they run. It's very important to cheer with each footfall you make as you run away. The thicker you lay it on and the happier you sound, the faster your dog will run to you. Try something like, "Good! Good! Wow! What a dog! Yay! Woo-hoo!" You will be amazed how much effort your dog makes in return.

- When she comes in for her treats, reward her close to your body, keeping your hands low to prevent jumping.

- Do not pat her head. Most dogs don't like to be leaned over or patted on the head, so you actually are not rewarding your dog for coming if you do this. Instead, praise her enthusiastically and feed her many treats in a row. Most dogs prefer this.

- When you're on a walk together, or hanging out in your fenced yard, keep your eye out for "check-ins." If she ever "checks in" with you of her own accord by looking up at you or coming up to you, make a big deal out of her and surprise her with a yummy treat. Make it worth her while to choose you over the rest of the environment.

Games to play to reinforce the "come" cue

If your dog is performing the step-by-step exercises well, start adding some games. Start indoors and work your way outside where there are more distractions. Only play these games for as long as your dog is eager for more (about five to ten minutes). Always end the game long before your dog gets bored.

Hide and seek

A helper holds your dog while you slowly, dramatically sneak off and hide. You then yell, "Fifi, find me!" The helper then releases your dog to come find you. Cheer and feed treats once your dog finds you. Make it easy at first until she gets the idea. First hide in the same room behind a chair, then try another room. If you don't have a helper, toss a treat away from you to get a head start while your dog goes after the treat. You can also initiate a surprise game of hide and seek any time your dog seems to be tuning you out. It works like a charm to get them keeping a better eye on you.

Ricochet recall

Two or three helpers stand about thirty feet apart, all of them holding special treats. Take turns saying, "Fifi, here!" then immediately cheer wildly so she'll want to come over to you. If she hesitates *even for a moment*, take off cheering in the opposite direction and she should come bounding after you. Feed her the treats when she catches up to you. To get her to "ricochet" to the next helper, withdraw your attention and the treats momentarily while the next person calls and cheers her over to them.

Mico has been given lots of rewards for coming when called, and it shows. Here he is doing a ricochet recall between his two people, who take turns calling and rewarding him for coming. Photo by Christopher Sims.

Chase

In a fenced-in yard, call your dog and then take off running. When your dog catches up to you, reward her with treats or a game of tug. Then take off in another direction. Be unpredictable! Never, ever, chase your dog; that's a great way to ruin your dog's responsiveness to "come."

Pez person

Every so often, ideally about a third of the time you practice your come cue, act like you are a human Pez dispenser when your dog reaches you after being called. Spend fifteen to thirty consecutive seconds dispensing treats, one at a time, lavishing praise on your dog all the while. You want your dog thinking, "Holy cow! She's turned into a human Pez dispenser. I never know when that might happen, so it always pays to come running lickety-split when I'm called!"

Gotcha

While not really a "come" game, playing this gotcha game will accustom your dog to having her collar grabbed once she comes to you. Many dogs have trouble learning to respond reliably to "come" because they anticipate the unpleasant sensation of having their collar grabbed once they reach the person who called them. Create a pleasant association with collar touch so your dog will be eager to come to you. Say, "gotcha," then grab her collar from underneath her chin, feed her treats, then release. Do this a few times in a row. Sometimes, while playing your "come" games, add in a little of the gotcha game.

Nose touch

The goal: You say, "touch!" and your dog swiftly bops the palm of your hand with her nose.

The benefits: you will be amazed at the many benefits that teaching "touch" has to offer. It takes only a few days to teach, but the benefits to you, your child, and your dog are astonishing. Teaching your dog to enthusiastically touch your palm with her nose on cue enables you to do all of the following:

- *Move the dog's face quickly away from your child,* even if you are all bunched up together. Stress builds (sometimes to the point of a bite) when dogs are crowded, their space is invaded, or they feel threatened and closed in. In everyday life this can happen even under the guidance of the best kid canine coach. If you see a warning sign, such as your dog looking away or flicking her tongue, you can flash the palm of your hand out to the side, away from your child, and cue "touch." Within seconds, your dog will have moved away from the stressful situation and toward your palm. You have provided her some breathing room and you will have prevented stress from escalating.

- *Move the dog across the room to you quickly.* Even dogs who have an excellent response to their "come" cue sometimes falter when we're only a few feet away, especially in a stressful situation. It's as though the dog is thinking, "What do you mean 'come'? I'm right here, you're right there. Duh." The "touch" prevents them from getting mentally "stuck" and gives them a specific target to head toward.

- *Create a pleasant association for the dog with children's hands,* which can be beneficial if rough handling should ever occur. First teach the "touch" cue to your dog, then teach your child and dog to practice "touch" together.

- *Give your child something appropriate and controlled to do with their hands*, which prevents stressful movements such as flailing, poking, hitting, or inadvertent rough handling. It's much easier for a child to be given a gentle, helpful task to do with his hands rather than just to insist that he stop touching incorrectly. A game of "touch" is a good alternative.

- *Accustom a rambunctious, mouthy dog to using his nose instead of teeth on hands*, though this should only be done under the supervision of a qualified dog trainer.

- *Teach a myriad of dog tricks*, like spin, rollover, sit pretty, weave through my legs as I walk, and many more. These are all much easier to teach if your dog responds enthusiastically to her "touch" cue.

Believe it or not, it will probably take you just a few sessions over a handful of days to teach the "touch" cue to your dog. Most dogs love this and catch on quickly. Some people find it helpful to practice first without the dog. After all, if you've got the moves down ahead of time, that makes the training go even faster.

Training session 1

Step 1
Prepare a handful of tiny, soft treats. Pea-sized bits of string cheese or commercial treats like Zuke's Power Bones are excellent choices. Do not choose treats that are hard or crunchy, or soft treats that are crumbly; the crumbs will end up on the floor or smeared on your hands, and this will confuse your dog and slow down the training process.

Step 2
Decide which hand will hold the treats. The other hand will be the "nose touch" hand and will not be used to hold or deliver any treats. You'll be switching hands in a later training session so that your dog will be able to execute "touch" to either of your hands. Just pick whichever hand you like to begin.

Step 3
Hide your clean "touch" hand behind your back. This will pique your dog's interest. Your dog may nuzzle the other hand holding the treats. Just ignore that and make a fist around the treats. In a moment your dog will learn how to get you to give her a treat.

Step 4
Present your rigidly flat palm out to your side, roughly at your dog's nose level. Say nothing. Just wait. Make sure your thumb is parallel to the ceiling; if your fingers are pointed down towards the floor, your dog might think you dropped a treat on the ground and become distracted looking for it.

Your dog will likely stretch toward your flat palm to investigate. If she puts herself into a sit position, make a few kissy noises so that she stands up. When you think about it, she's very clever to try this at first. You've been working hard on sit and "say please," so this has become her default behavior. What a good girl! However, for this exercise, ignore it when she sits and move around a bit if necessary to keep her standing. She cannot sit and successfully reach for your hand with her nose at the same time, so make sure she's standing.

Step 5
When she bumps your hand with her nose, keep your touch hand right where it is as you say "yes" and deliver a treat with your other hand. For the best, fastest results, place the treat as close as possible to the spot where your dog bopped your palm and let your dog take the treat at that spot. We want her thinking, "Hmmm, something about bopping the palm of her hand makes good things happen."

Step 6
Repeat steps 3-6 three to five times in a row. Congratulations! You've completed your first touch training session. Allow your dog's brain to rest at least a couple of hours before trying again.

Training session 2
In session two, you will teach your dog to nose touch your palm even if your hand shifts to different positions.

Step 1
Prepare a handful of treats as in session 1.

Step 2
Use the same touch hand as in session 1, but hide it behind your back to create interest.

Step 3
Flash your touch palm in the same location as in session 1.

Hold your hand steady, palm at nose-level with the dog, fingers parallel to the floor.
Photo by author.

Step 4

When your dog bops your palm with her nose, instantly say "yes" and reward her with a treat from your other hand, just as before.

Step 5

Repeat the above steps, but for the next five repetitions, move your touch hand to slightly different positions. Try moving it a few inches to your left or right. Try sitting, standing, and crouching. End on a successful nose touch. You've completed session 2!

Training session 3
Practice as in session 2.

Training session 4
Practice as in session 2, but in a new room, continuing to vary your touch hand position by a few inches in all directions. Remember to encourage your dog to remain in a standing position, by backing up briskly and making kissy noises if necessary. If it's very easy for your dog to succeed, try switching hands.

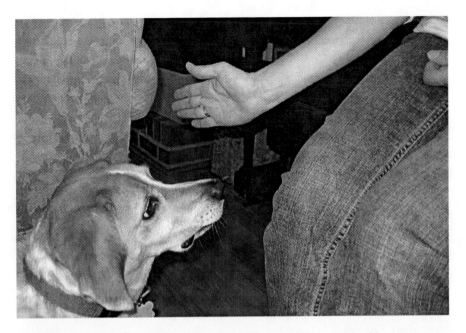

Wait quietly for the dog to move toward your palm.

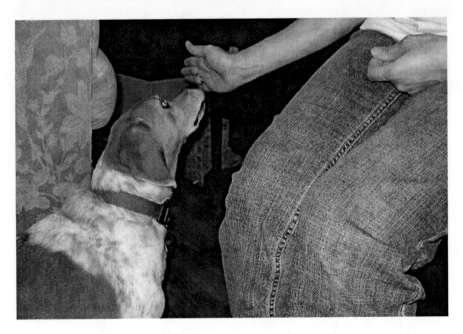

When her nose bumps your palm, say "yes" and feed her a treat. Once she begins doing this consistently when she sees your palm held out, add a verbal signal by saying, "Fifi, touch!" just before you flash your palm. Photos by author.

Training session 5

If you haven't already tried switching hands, start session 5 with the opposite hand serving as your nose touch hand. Be patient, as this means going back to square one for your dog. Remember: she thinks one of the hands is now a magic lever that makes treats appear from the other. Be sure to deliver the treat with the opposite hand, as closely as possible to where your dog's nose touched your palm.

Practice every day for three to five minutes at a time. Once your dog eagerly performs a nose touch, on either hand, regardless of the position of your hand, it's time for the big leagues!

The big leagues: Training session 1

Prepare the treats as above. Keep your hand behind your back. Then, right before (not during, not after) you flash your nose touch hand from behind, say pleasantly, "Fifi, touch!" Then, and not before, flash your palm as usual. Practice as above, repeating your verbal cue only once for each new nose touch repetition.

The big leagues: Training session 2

Using your new verbal cue, start asking your dog for a nose touch. Introduce the following variables: (As always, remember to be quick with your word "yes" at the instant of each nose touch and reward with a treat. The only exception to this is a more advanced, multiple touch exercise listed below.)

- Move further away from your dog, a few feet at a time.

- Sit on a piece of furniture.

- Sit on the floor.

- Try it in another room.

- Vary which hand you use.

- Advanced: Try asking for two nose touches in a row before
  you say "yes" and feed her a treat. If that's easy, try for
  three in a row. Now you can vary the number of nose
  touches your dog performs in a row.

The finished product
- Say, "Fifi, touch."

- Present the palm of your hand.

- When the dog touches your palm firmly with his nose say "yes."

- Feed her a treat (keep them stored in little tins throughout the house).

- Eventually you'll reward her with a treat only occasionally (for example, when your dog performs "touch" in challenging situations). Otherwise, offer praise instead of saying yes and feeding a treat.

Practice while sitting on the couch with your child and dog present, standing in the kitchen, and out in the yard. That way it will come easily to you and you'll react more quickly should you observe your dog give warning signs of stress.

If you master the three exercises in this section, check out the games section in chapter 3 to start teaching some tricks! See the appendix for information on an excellent training video and how to find a professional dog trainer. If you haven't trained your dog in a while, you'll be amazed at how smart he still is! Keeping his training sharp is good for his mental health, your mental health, and for your child's safety.

Baby = Good!

Isn't it amazing how you can change your dog's mood just by reaching for his leash? You probably didn't teach him that on purpose. Just the visual trigger of the leash in your hand is enough to fill him with glee, because it is a consistent tip-off that he'll be going for a walk. Other objects or smells may trigger feelings of fear or anger. The sight of toenail trimmers, for example, probably does not make your dog feel happy. It only takes a few repetitions for the dog to make an emotional association like these: leash = good, toenail trimmers = bad.

Naturally, we want your dog to make the association baby = good. Soon your baby will bring all kinds of wondrous sounds, scents, and visual experiences into your dog's life. Ideally these will be triggers for pleasant emotions, rather than triggers for irritation, fear, or anger. Certainly it is worthwhile to try to make your dog's impressions of these baby-related experiences good ones. If the smells, movements, and touch associated with the baby make your dog feel calm and pleasant, then you will help your dog have a favorable impression of your baby. A client of mine is expecting a baby. She and her partner started working on creating a pleasant association with baby-related things. Now even when they say the word "baby" the dog wags her tail!

Sadie learns to happily control herself when attention is lavished on the baby. Mom feeds her a treat to teach her that their attention to the baby equates to good things for Sadie. Photo by author.

When to get help

Get professional help if your dog has ever growled, struggled or used his teeth or mouth in response to being touched, petted, having his paws wiped off or groomed. If your dog regularly gets ear or eye cleanings or medicines, please get professional help so your dog will not be wary about having his ears touched. One day, your child will probably try to reach for your dog's ears or paws, so don't leave it to chance.

Your dog perceives the world through his senses. He is especially aware of scents, sounds, movements, and touch. Below you'll find a list of things from each of these sensory categories (plus an important bonus category: attention to the baby). About three weeks before your baby arrives, pick things from two categories each day, and actively create a positive association with those things for your dog using some of the suggestions from the list. If you think of the leash, you created a positive association with your dog's leash by first showing the leash, then walking the dog. Soon the dog was feeling leash = good. So the first thing to do is expose your dog to some new baby-related object or experience, and then offer him something he likes, like treats. The new experience becomes the tip-off for feeling good.

- · scent: lotions, powders, diapers, friends' children, blanket from the hospital

- · sound: recorded CDs of babies and children playing, baby talk directed at a doll, playground sounds, electronic toys, squeaky toys, musical sounds

- · movement: crawling baby toy, mechanical swing, running children, playground activity, t-ball or soccer game, bikes and roller skates going by

- touch: Pair child-like touch with treats. Start easy and work up to gently grabbing a toe or ear. Touch the tail, then feed a treat. Touch a toe, then feed a treat. Give a light hug, then give five treats one at a time, praising calmly and generously. This is a safety measure in case someone forgets and touches the dog inappropriately.

- attention to baby: Spend time in nursery, carry and fuss over a doll, pretend to change a diaper, carry a doll around in a car seat. While you are engaging in these activities with the doll, your dog should play with a food stuffed Kong, or receive attention, treats or massage from your spouse. This way your dog associates your attention to the baby with happy feelings. Trade roles with your spouse the next time you practice. Pay less attention to your dog when there is no baby doll being played with. This gives your dog the idea that attention to the baby equates with good things for him. Occasionally put your dog in the safety zone with a special edible yummy (like a stuffed Kong) while you play with the doll in the next room; get your dog used to the idea of overhearing baby sounds in the next room.

Planned, happy, training sessions with real kids is especially important if a child older than an infant is joining your family. To teach your dog that the tip-off for feeling good is toddlers or older kids running around screeching and flailing their little arms, enlist the help of some friends, nieces, and local playgrounds, and be sure to bring some wonderful treats.

A sample schedule would be to choose two scents and two movements to work on for Monday. On Tuesday, pick two types of touch and two sounds, and so on. Spend three to five minutes on each one, which will mean four very quick sessions a day. Mealtime is a great opportunity for this. If you present the new experience and then present a meal, you will easily integrate two of the four sessions into your day. For example:

- Rub some baby lotion on your hands or forearms before you feed your dog. Doing so will create a positive association with one of the baby's scents.

- Set the mechanical swing on low and then give your dog a little bit of his dinner at a time until it's all gone, then turn off the swing.

Happy Kids, Happy Dogs

- Turn the baby sounds CD on low volume, then feed your dog his meal.

- Instead of feeding breakfast out of a bowl, visit a neighborhood park and, when your dog notices a running child, feed him part of his breakfast. (Since you want an extra happy association with the combination of scent, sound, and movement generated by the kids at the playground, mix in some extra special morsels, like bits of string cheese.)

What if treats send your dog over the top? If treats make your dog go totally bonkers, you need to back up a step and teach him some impulse control. Your dog has inadvertently been taught that getting wound up is rewarded with treats. So teach your dog that calm is what earns goodies:

- Use more boring training treats to begin with, such as using your dog's regular food bits rather than, say, roast beef.

- Stay calm and quiet yourself while you're delivering the treat. Keep your hands still.

- Reward calm behavior when your dog just happens to offer it. This means walking around with kibble in your pockets, so that you can slip your dog a goodie when he's just lying there, relaxing.

- Never feed the dog a treat or his dinner if he's dancing around in wild anticipation, barking, or whining. Wait until he's sitting calmly, then reach for the food. Withdraw your hand or leave the room if he resumes his antics. He will soon figure out that calm behavior equates to food, and that food represents a chance to show off calm behavior.

- If your dog truly relishes a massage or a thorough chin scratching, use gentle, calm touch like that to reward him instead of treats.

As already mentioned, one day your dog may be faced with a child (either your own or a visiting child) who tries to hug him, take a toy away, or touch him unexpectedly. Accustom your dog to these things ahead of time; doing so may help avoid an aggressive episode. Take a toy, then feed him a treat. Give him a hug, then feed him a treat. Gently

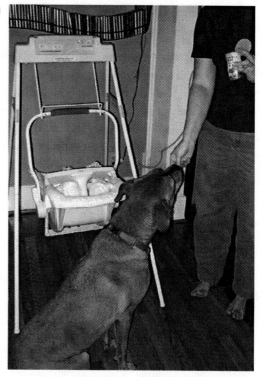

Hannah feeds Sadie treats for sitting calmly while the baby doll rocks back and forth in the mechanical swing. Photo by author.

grasp his tail, then feed him a treat. Gently grasp an ear or a paw, then feed him a treat. However, remember that these are exercises designed for people-oriented dogs who have not shown warning signs of stress associated with them in the past. For other types of dogs, you should see a qualified dog expert to obtain a customized plan.

Your efforts to maintain your dog's happy association with your child will continue for years. Every time your child does something new, you'll be there to praise your dog or offer gentle petting, or change the situation to make it easier for your dog and child to get along. The remaining time you have before the baby arrives may be the last chance you have to work on these associations at your own pace, with no surprises thrown in. So take advantage of it and create many planned, happy exposures to the sight, sounds, scent, and touch of children.

Chapter 2:
Introducing Your Baby and Your Dog

What to Do the Day You Bring Your Baby Home

When it comes to building a successful relationship between your child and your dog, the most meaningful time and effort you invest should come before the baby's arrival and during each interaction as the child grows. Their actual introduction is but a fleeting moment. If you practice the main points of the meeting ahead of time it should go fine. Rather than worrying too much about this one moment, invest your energy in the interactions that will come afterward. That is where your time will be best spent.

Having said that, there are certainly things you can do to help ensure that the moment your dog meets your baby goes smoothly. Simply rehearse the introduction ahead of time, using a doll as a stand-in for your baby. Start two weeks before the baby's arrival and practice a few days a week. If your dog is super-rambunctious, you'll need to start sooner and practice more often. It's best to have the mother take the lead for this exercise, as the dog will be especially eager to greet her after she returns home from the hospital. Here's what to do:

- Enter the room carrying a baby-scented item like a blanket (but not the doll), ask your dog to sit, and greet her calmly.

- Reward your dog with treats and/or calm praise and touch. (If your dog gets up from the sit, turn your back and exit. Try again and reward your dog for a shorter duration sit.)

- Have helper enter holding a baby doll.

- Sit in a firm chair (such as at the table, not a big, low chair), and take the doll from your helper.

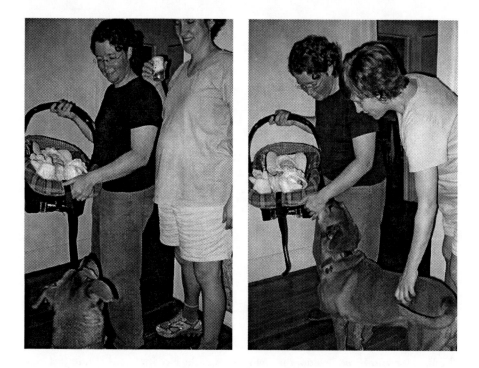

Left: Sadie sits to ask to greet mom. Right: Sadie is eager to meet the baby. Notice Sadie's curved body and low, sweeping tail wag. She is calmly seeking out affection with this gentle body language. Photos by author.

- Give your dog treats and slow, gentle petting for sitting calmly near you.

- Your dog may investigate and sniff the doll while being petted.

- The helper should then release your dog from the sit and continue to monitor her while you stand and walk with the baby doll.

Important tips

- Get a friend or dog walker to aerobically exercise your dog early on the day your baby is coming home and beyond. If possible, begin this routine a week or more before the big day. Remember: A tired dog is a good dog.

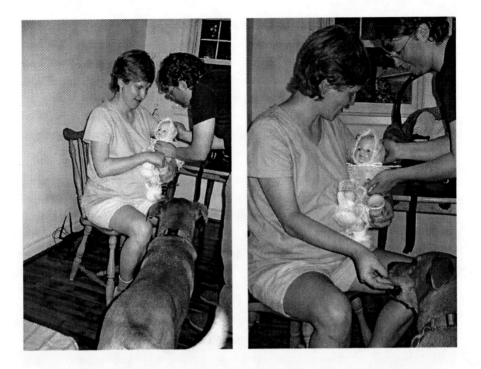

Left: Practicing with a doll, mom sits at the table in preparation for introducing Sadie to the baby. Right: Sadie receives calm petting, a treat, and low-key praise for sitting beside mom and the baby. Photos by author.

- Look for wiggly greeting behavior from your dog when she meets the new baby. This is ideal. She will be curious, which is normal. Sniffing is fine. Just make sure your dog is sitting and investigating in a calm, controlled manner. Your dog may lick at your baby's feet. A few affectionate licks on the feet are fine as long as your dog is very calm and gentle, but if you'd rather she didn't lick, just remind the dog to sit, then praise her calmly. This is no time to reprimand your dog, yank on her collar, or shove her away. Remember: you want her to equate the presence of the baby with good things for her.

- Practice ahead of time and generously reward calm, polite behavior.

Warning Signs and What to Do about Them

Stiffening, silent staring, obsessive whining and pacing, or other agitated behavior by your dog toward your baby or the baby's resting place are very serious. While these signs are very, very rare, they may indicate that your dog is registering your baby as prey. If your dog exhibits any of these signs or exhibits any other behavior that makes you feel strange, do not make excuses for him or let him get close to your baby. Always err on side of caution. Have a friend take your dog for the night while you consult with a professional referred to you by your veterinarian.

Please note that just because your dog doesn't exhibit behavior that "looks aggressive" does not mean that it is ever okay to leave your dog and child unattended. Millions of children are bitten by dogs every year. If you can't imagine how quickly a bite can occur, consider that, while I was writing this book, in Rhode Island a six-day-old baby girl was killed in her portable crib by the family dog when her mother turned her back just for an instant to get something from the kitchen. In Colorado, another mother was making mud pies in the backyard with her five-year-old daughter and their two dogs; she went inside just for a few moments to get some juice and returned to find her daughter had been killed. My heart goes out to these families. Please don't ever leave your child unattended with your dog. Ever. The chance of your child being killed is extraordinarily slim, but the chance of a bite is great, and it can happen very quickly. Use the safety zone or take the dog or child with you into the other room. Get into this habit from the very moment you introduce your baby and your dog.

Frequently Asked Questions about Dogs and Infants

The following are some of the questions most frequently asked by expectant parents in the prenatal seminars I conduct at hospitals:

"Is it ok if the dog licks the baby?"

If your dog is relaxed while you hold the baby in your arms, you may allow him to come a bit closer to sniff and even to gently lick at the baby's blanketed feet. Provided that your dog is calm and under control, normal investigating is a good thing. It is much better to encourage gentle social behavior than to pull or shove the dog away from your baby each time he approaches to get to know the new family member. If you get tense and upset at the dog each time he wishes to get closer to the baby, you may inadvertently teach him to associate the baby with feeling bad. It would be more productive to examine why you are feeling so tense. Perhaps the dog is showing warning signs, or perhaps you just need a better plan and some time to practice.

Practice ahead of time so your dog is calm and under control for greeting the baby. There's no need for a wound-up dog to be licking a newborn. In fact, it tends to make everyone a little jumpy. Gently remind the dog to sit if he starts to get overly excited. This strategy will help him regroup without causing tension or making him feel isolated. As an important bonus, he will hear, "good boy!" for sitting in the presence of your new baby.

"Can we just leave our dog out in the yard, making the yard the safety zone?"

Some dogs do fine when left unattended in the backyard, provided there is a secure fence that they cannot see through. However, a fenced yard does not make a good safety zone. The purpose of the safety zone is not to isolate your dog. The safety zone should be a cozy, indoor place near you. That way your dog can still hear and smell you, while taking a break from the action. There are some common problems that result from isolating a dog outside in the yard, including:

- barking

- climbing or jumping over the fence

- digging

- stress-induced behavior, like pacing

- stress-induced self mutilation caused by excessive licking of paws or other body parts

- arousal and aggression toward passersby.

If your dog is left in the yard for prolonged periods of time, he may also be taunted by people, especially kids, who may even throw things at him. A fenced yard is not a good place for a dog to be isolated. However, it can be a good place for your dog and your child to play, train, and relax together, but only under the attentive eyes of a kid canine coach.

If you do have a fenced-in yard, I recommend using a fence that does not harm or frighten your dog, or cause unintended fallout such as aggression, shyness, housetraining problems, or mistrust of people. Instead of using an electric shock fence, consider fencing off a small area of your yard with green wire garden fencing (available at large home improvement stores) or a fence like those offered online by Best Friend Fence, which are made of sturdy, black plastic mesh.

If you're planning on having your dog spend most of his time outside because you're concerned about his behavior (toward adults or children), I strongly recommend you consult the appendix to get the help of a qualified dog behavior expert. Even the most diligently executed prevention strategies fail at some point. Get help now before the problem gets worse or someone gets hurt.

"My dog doesn't care about food or treats, but I want to use them to create a pleasant association with our baby. Is there anything we can do?"

If your dog is blasé about treats, there are several things you can do.

1. Make sure she is fed on a strict schedule. This means giving your dog fifteen minutes to eat, then removing the bowl whether it is empty or not. Free feeding, in which your dog helps herself from the food bowl throughout the day, is not recommended for most dogs.

2. Use high quality treats, such as real cheese, tofu dogs, or macaroni noodles cooked in chicken broth. Use tiny, pea-sized pieces and be generous. (To prevent begging, never feed your dog from the table.)

3. Initiate training sessions when your dog is looking forward to a meal, not just after she's finished her supper.

"My dog gets overly excited around treats. How can we train him for calm behavior when he gets so worked up over the treats?"

If your dog is a real spaz when treats come out, then that may be an indication that he's been routinely rewarded for spazzy behavior in the presence of treats. Even a dog who is super-duper happy about food will behave in a controlled, polite way if that is the type of behavior that you reward. After all, dogs do what works. To help your dog learn to be calm around treats, follow these steps:

1. Put your dog's leash on him and let him drag it around the room. This way you can step on the leash and regain control should he get rowdy.

2. Take a whole handful of relatively ho-hum treats, like bits of stale bread or dry dog food, in your hand.

3. Don't ask your dog to do a darned thing. Be silent. If he starts losing his marbles and jumping all over, step on the leash so that if he jumps he can't clamber all over you. Naturally he should wear a fabric or other soft collar. It's not supposed to hurt, it's just supposed to prevent him from jumping. If he paws or mouths at your hands, fold your arms. This teaches him that spazzy dog behavior makes you turn into a mannequin, unable to feed dog treats.

4. At some point your dog will stop for a second to reevaluate the situation: "Why is she ignoring me? How can I get her to give me the treat?" At that moment, while he is still, you will quietly say "yes," and feed him one piece of dog food. The word "yes" in this situation is not a command. It is a precise marker of what your dog has just done to earn a treat. It lets him know that controlling himself is what earned him the treat.

5. After two or three minutes of you rewarding calm behavior and acting like a mannequin in response to rowdy behavior, your dog will figure out the system. He will start offering you calmer, more self-controlled behavior. Be quick to say "yes" and then feed him a treat each time he offers something other than leaping and snorting.

6. Practice no more than three times a day. By the second or third session, your dog will probably start offering a sit all on his own. Say "yes" and feed him a treat.

7. In subsequent sessions, gradually build up to longer moments of still, calm behavior before you say "yes" and feed the treat.

I highly recommend instituting "say please" with your dog for real-life rewards like a walk or some petting. This will help him learn to calm himself without you having to bug him about it. Saying please in this way will enable him to control his own impulses, rather than you doing all the work to control him.

If your dog grabs treats roughly, or is so excited about food that he stiffens or growls when you reach for the food, consult a qualified dog trainer for advice tailored to your dog. The sooner you intervene with professional help, the better.

"My dog goes nuts for squeaky toys. How will this work with squeaky baby toys in the house?"

Dogs are predators, and so their getting excited about squeaky toys is totally normal. Their behavior is similar to how they would chase and bite real-life prey. Therefore, I recommend getting this under control as soon as possible. Start with the following rules:

· Dogs who sit when asked may then chase the dog squeaky toy with permission.

- Dogs who do a down-stay may get the dog squeaky toy with permission.

- Dogs who do a "come" or "touch" (see the cues section in chapter 1) when they hear a squeaky toy are rewarded with a special food treat.

Keep your child's toys picked up or designate a baby toy area with a baby gate.

"My dog seems pretty well behaved. How do I know what to work on?"

Introduce the changes in routine and baby smells, sounds, and movements described in chapter 1. Implementing "say please" is mentally enriching and fun for most dogs. Plan to make sure that your dog has pleasant experiences around children of all ages starting now. Most of all, appreciate what a great dog you have, but do not take her for granted. Assume she needs a little help. Help her to succeed by coaching your child in correct behavior. Praise and reward both of them for interacting pleasantly together.

"Is there a way to teach our dog to differentiate between baby toys and dog toys? I just have a feeling it is going to be a battle to keep her from taking the baby's toys. I have not let her have any plush toys, but if she ever finds a stuffed animal she seems to think it's hers. I have tried to tell her no and then give her a dog toy, but it does not stop her."

Give your dog's toys a special scent so that she will learn to identify her toys and begin to prefer them over baby toys. Apply just a dab of meat juice to the toys you want your dog to grab. You may also get a few baby toys soon, and put just a tiny dab of perfume or Listerine (the older, light brown kind) on them. She will likely avoid them. (You could also do that with your baby's real toys; your baby wouldn't notice a tiny dab, but your dog would.) The main thing is to apply a scent your dog loves to her dog toys so that she will learn which toys you want to her choose. This is important also because the baby toys will soon outnumber the dog toys, and it's much easier to indicate what you do want your dog grabbing than to mark each baby toy.

You mention the strategy of telling your dog no if she grabs a baby toy and then giving her an appropriate dog toy. The reason I don't recommend that is that it could easily teach her that she gets attention for nabbing plush toys. Dogs are very clever, so it wouldn't take much to get her to come to that conclusion. If your child is playing with a plush toy, and your dog heads toward her to grab it, instantly call your dog to you instead and reward her for coming. Then give her something better to do so she won't obsess about the plush toy your child has (tethering her with a stuffed Kong comes to mind). If you are consistent, your dog will likely start anticipating this pattern and come to you automatically when she sees your child has a toy. Sometimes this new behavior happens after only a handful of repetitions. While this works with most dogs, if your dog is ultra enthusiastic about plush toys it is perfectly okay to use the safety zone at times when your child is holding a particularly tempting toy.

Finally, you could give your dog an outlet for her plush toy enthusiasm with some distinctly doggie plush toys, like rope toys or even a dog plush toy or two that are marked with the meat scent. I recommend keeping these in a special place so she doesn't have unlimited access to them (otherwise she may learn that any plush toy on the floor is fair game). You could offer her the chance to play with these special toys on occasion, perhaps even in a special place like outside with you.

"If I say "good boy" to my baby, how will my dog know I'm not talking to him?"

Scientific studies indicate what you've probably experienced with your own dog: dogs are amazingly perceptive of human social cues. One researcher even found that dogs are better than chimpanzees at picking up social cues from humans. So if you're leaning over the crib, soothing your baby, your dog will likely not become confused. If you're interacting with your baby, your dog will figure that out, just as he can usually tell when your words are directed at another person or dog. I recommend practicing cooing at and interacting with a baby doll starting a couple of weeks before the due date so that your dog gets used to you lavishing affection on a newcomer in the household.

"We have two dogs. How do we prepare them? Will they compete to be near the baby or us?"

The main thing is to prepare ahead of time. You should make sure both dogs are having their daily needs met, and make any necessary changes now. They should be getting enough aerobic exercise, and both should "say please" for everything they receive. Polish up "come" and the "nose touch." If one of your dogs competes with the other for your attention, work with a qualified trainer to teach both how to show self control while the other receives affection. This is especially important for dogs who cut off other dogs or people from affectionate moments with you. In my experience, dogs who are in the habit of jostling each other out of the way to compete for your affection may view a small child as a rival for your attention as well.

"One of us thinks the dog is fine the way he is, but the other is concerned. What should we do?"

You don't have to agree. If either of you thinks your dog needs a little extra help, get help from a qualified trainer. If you contact a professional trainer and it turns out that your dog does not need professional help, there will be no harm done (as long as you go with a gentle, qualified trainer). There are enough things coming your way for which there is really no way to prepare. You might as well enjoy the peace of mind knowing you did everything you could have ahead of time to help your dog, your child, and yourselves.

"Our dog is aggressive toward other dogs. He even guards toys or food from other dogs. Does this mean he will be aggressive with the baby?"

If your dog does not get along well with other dogs, your child may or may not be at a greater risk of injury. There is no good data on whether or not dog-on-dog aggression is predictive of dog-on-child aggression. However, my philosophy is to err on the side of caution. Some dogs who react aggressively when other dogs get too close to them have no trouble at all with a person doing the same thing. Some dogs do not share their toys or food with other dogs but don't mind a person coming near them when they have something they value. Some dogs do fine with other dogs playing off leash, but demonstrate aggression when they are on a leash walk.

In my personal and professional experience, dogs who have little tolerance for other dogs competing for space, toys, or attention can also have low tolerance for little children in these same situations. Dogs who are aggressive toward other dogs on leash can be hard to manage. This can be risky for you and your child, especially if your dog lunges toward another dog while you are walking with him and your baby. See the appendix for a list of resources to help you find a qualified professional to assess your dog and recommend training and safety options.

"Our dog paws at us when she wants us to pet her, and we worry that our baby will be scratched. How do we stop her from doing this?"

This is a good observation. What might feel like only a strong nudge to you might scrape or upset your child. Your dog is likely doing this to get a reaction from you, and you likely do react, otherwise she would have abandoned this strategy long ago. Sometimes you may react by talking to your dog. Sometimes you may pat her or reprimand her. If so, from your dog's perspective, pawing at you is often an effective way of getting attention from you of one sort or another.

From now on, have your dog "say please" for everything she wants. This includes petting and attention from you. Call her to you for petting when you want to pet her. Otherwise, refrain from absent-minded petting or stroking. When she saunters up to you with that gleam in her eye, don't wait to see what she will do next; ask her to sit and then reward her with some pleasant attention and petting. Keep her calm by touching her slowly and using a calm, low-pitched voice. If she paws at you, instantly stand and leave the room. Each person in the household must agree to this plan. Some dogs figure out after only a few repetitions that you will gladly give your attention to them for polite sitting, but that they lose you altogether for using their paws. Instead of a sit, you can ask for a nose touch as your dog approaches. It is very difficult for a dog to paw at you while leaning forward with her nose. This can help break her of the pawing habit by replacing it with something gentler that still gets your attention.

"We are expecting our first child and my parents are excited to be grandparents. However, when it comes to their dog, we are worried about how he will act around our child. When we try to raise the topic with them they dismiss our concerns and insist their dog is perfect. How can we get them to take our concerns seriously?"

If this is a source of tension for you all, try talking about it again. Emphasize that you'd like their dog and your child to be friends, and that you'd like to talk about having some basic precautions in place to make that outcome likelier. Be prepared to accept that they may not like the idea of setting up a safety zone in their house for their dog, and they may not understand that you plan to take your child out of the room sometimes to give their dog a break. In addition to that conversation, I recommend doing three things to ease your mind. First, accept that you cannot control your parents' or in-laws' behavior, but you can make decisions to keep your child safer. Second, do what you need to do in order to feel your child is safe at your parents' or in-laws' house. Think of it this way: imagine that your parents would refuse to block their stairways with baby gates when your toddler visited. How would you handle that? Third, when you visit your parents

Happy Kids, Happy Dogs

with your child, use the kid canine coaching techniques to encourage correct behavior in your child and to monitor stress signals in your parents' dog. You may even want to identify signs of dog stress out loud if your parents are interested in learning about them ("I notice that Rover is showing some common signs of dog stress that we've learned about. He's avoiding the baby and he's flicking his tongue."). Then ask if the dog could be confined in another room for some nap time or chew toy time.

Chapter 3:
Your Growing and Changing Child

The Three Principles for Successfully Nurturing Child-Dog Relationships

When it comes to their child and their dog, most parents want to keep things as simple as possible. They want their dog to be happy and well-behaved. They want their child to be happy, respectful, and safe. Fortunately it doesn't take a lot of fancy dog training to achieve these goals, but it does require putting into practice three basic principles:

1. Meet your dog's daily needs for aerobic exercise, affection, and training.

2. Actively coach your child and dog through their interactions.

3. Use the safety zone when you are too tired or too busy to coach.

These three principles, meeting your dog's daily needs, being an effective kid canine coach, and using the safety zone, form the essential foundation for good child-dog relationships.

Let's talk about the first principle. Your dog needs plenty of physical and mental exercise every day, as well as affection given to him when he's calm and quiet. If he does not receive these, the consequence may be annoying dog behaviors like hyperactivity, destructive chewing, barking, and other more serious behaviors. Often people say they don't have the time or energy to exercise their dog. Here are some ideas for meeting your dog's aerobic exercise needs that my clients have found useful:

- Play fetch in your fenced yard, or indoors if you have a small dog.

- Take a brisk walk with your baby in the stroller.

- Hire a dog walker.

- Enroll in doggie daycare a couple of days a week.

- Teach your dog to chase a favorite toy on a string (cat-style) and to release the toy on cue (keep the toy on the ground to prevent injury).

- Arrange play dates with other neighborhood dogs.

- Walk your dog in a new location, like a new park or an unfamiliar neighborhood (this can be very stimulating and tiring, even if it's only a fifteen-minute outing).

- Match your dog up with a neighbor or college student looking for a jogging buddy.

You may use any combination of the above suggestions, but remember that each dog is different, so you should consult with your veterinarian about exercise or with a dog trainer for mental games for your pooch. To meet your dog's needs for mental stimulation, have your dog sit before she gets or does anything. Feed meals via food dispensing puzzle toys instead of out of a bowl. Affection, in the form of relaxing grooming or petting for a few minutes, is a nice way to spend quality time together while your partner plays with the baby and once the baby's gone to bed for the night.

To prepare your child and your dog to succeed, start by making sure you are meeting your dog's daily needs for exercise, mental stimulation, and affection. In the next sections we'll talk about how to teach your child what to do and what not to do around your dog, and how to recognize potentially dangerous signs of stress in your dog.

Dos and Don'ts for Child Behavior

Children are adorable. Dogs are adorable. When we see them together, it is hard to resist feeling that all is right with the world. Advertisers have noticed this, too, and use it to sell products. After all, it would hardly be effective advertising to show actors using toilet paper or diapers for what they are intended! As a viewer, it's much more pleasant to watch a puppy and a baby, to feel happy, and to notice the roll of toilet paper resting nearby. That sells toilet paper. Therefore, the child-plus-dog formula is all over television.

Strictly for research purposes, I watched television to see how children and dogs are portrayed together. Within a half-hour of watching, I saw five commercials that depicted child-dog interactions. All of them showed improper situations that put the children at risk for a bite. Watch the commercials of any given daytime television program (I highly recommend a soap opera for this purpose) and see how many times you see a scene in which a child hugs a dog, a toddler charges up to a dog, children dress a dog in an outfit, or a dog tries to move away and the child runs after him. These images are used to make us feel all touchy-feely so that we will have a happy association with the toilet paper or the diapers and in turn go purchase them. But the images have nothing to do with real life. You can tell because the one thing you will not see is an adult managing the situation and guiding the children and dog toward the correct behavior.

On television and in the movies, children and dogs seem to coexist almost magically. No knowledgeable adult is ever depicted actively coaching the children, and there is plenty of inappropriate handling of the dogs. With so many children and adults watching these media images, full of the absolute wrong ways to touch and interact with dogs, it is no wonder so few people know the dos and don'ts of child-dog interactions. In this section you'll learn the dos and don'ts for children when they interact with a dog. They are designed to help keep your child safe and to prevent your dog from developing bad feelings toward your child.

Dos

There are many important safety rules parents teach their children: Don't touch the electrical outlet. Don't touch the stove. Don't hit other children. Cross the street only like this. Only go with a stranger in certain circumstances. It takes effort to teach these, but it's worth the effort to prevent stress and injury.

Child-dog interactions are in the same category. Your child is depending on you to teach the correct way to be safe from the very beginning. Children are at the greatest risk of being bitten by their own dogs. Plus, other dogs are everywhere: at a friend or family member's house, around the neighborhood, at a soccer game. Children who have dogs at home tend to be fearless around all dogs, an attitude which places them at greater risk when visiting relatives or neighbors who have a dog. Your child is counting on you to teach them the correct way to show affection, respect, and kindness to dogs. Model the correct way to do it each time you interact with any dog, including your own. It is part of your job as a parent and as a dog owner.

Provided the dog shows no stress signs and has no history of behavior problems, under adult coaching children may:

- greet the dog, in the safest way (see below)

- help teach or show off the dog's tricks and obedience cues

- offer gentle, slow petting on the side of the dog's face and under the chin

- give the dog a kiss by kissing their hand and then gently petting the dog with that hand

- play find-it games (see the games section for examples)

- bake dog cookies (look for easy recipes on-line)

- help groom, feed, or give water to the dog

- help play fetch with the dog

- help take the dog for walks (while the adult should always hold the leash, for fun use a double-handled leash so the child can hold on, too)

- sing quietly to the dog

- count the dog's spots, feet, ears, tail, eyes, and legs

- draw pictures of the dog

- play indoor and outdoor games with the dog (see the games section in this chapter for specific ideas)

- learn to pick up a puppy correctly (for kids ages five and up).

This last point deserves particular attention. Please be aware that most puppies feel frightened, and even bite defensively, when picked up by children. The reason is that most children don't have the strength, coordination, and know-how to do it correctly. Puppies are only small enough to be picked up by kids for a short time in their lives, but this is during a developmental stage in which potentially lasting associations are made with your child. (If your puppy avoids your child or gets nippy, put a moratorium on your child picking up the puppy until you get professional guidance.)

Please prevent your well-meaning child from inadvertently sabotaging his friendship with the puppy by lifting him incorrectly. The best thing would be for kids not to pick up the puppy, but this is nearly impossible to implement consistently. I can't say I blame the kids. After all, who can resist an adorable puppy? This is where you need to be proactive. Help the puppy feel safe around your child by showing your child how to lift the puppy correctly: supporting the puppy's back end with one hand and forearm under the tail, while supporting the puppy's chest with the other hand (never grasp the front end alone or the front legs or elbows). The puppy should be held upright and close to the child's chest, not cradled like a baby. Your child should hold the puppy in his or her lap, not wander around holding the puppy. To put him down, the puppy should be placed gently on the ground, all four feet touching down softly at once. Since it's very difficult to prevent the puppy being picked up, it's best to turn things to everyone's advantage by teaching the correct, gentle method. Most kids think it's pretty neat to be entrusted with such an important responsibility.

The correct way to hold a puppy. This puppy is almost too large to pick up, which is similar to how it feels to a child learning to hold a smaller puppy. Photo by author.

Don'ts

Dogs are not people. This simple fact is incredibly important to acknowledge. The way people show affection to other people just happens to involve gestures that most dogs find threatening. Believe it or not, most of the ways people show affection to dogs is interpreted by dogs as unpleasant and even threatening.

Try to imagine things from your dog's point of view by putting yourself in a similar situation. If you found yourself on the planet Zorg, and your lovely, well-meaning Zorg host family showed you Zorg affection by walking up to you and giving your forehead a firm flick, you'd get quite bent out of shape. To our dogs, most human actions seem as appropriate as we would find this sort of Zorg affection. Yet we humans have gotten in the habit of doing various well-meaning but threatening things to our dogs, assuming that a "good dog" will just accept it. Such behavior is everywhere you look. Countless images in feel-good TV ads and movies show someone hugging a dog or putting their face in a dog's face. Like most half-baked things we see on TV, the underlying message of these images should be, "Don't try this at home!"

Do not allow your child to do any of the following, by accident or on purpose. In fact, don't do any of these things yourself, because it would mean modeling the wrong behavior for your child, and modeling the wrong behavior could put your child at risk with your dog or a neighbor's dog.

- hugging
- kissing
- pinching
- poking
- wrestling
- rough play
- running
- screaming
- teasing
- straddling or riding
- chasing
- following
- blowing at

- touching from behind

- touching with an object (doll, toy, stick, etc)

- hitting or kicking, even slightly

- pulling or holding ears or tail

- pulling hair

- grabbing paws

- "dancing" by holding paws

- using the dog to help stand up

- leaning or lying on the dog

- dressing the dog in outfits or hats

- disturbing or interacting with a dog who is confined (in a car, a crate, behind a baby gate, tied outside a store, etc.)

- approaching a dog who is resting or sleeping

- approaching a dog who is on his/her dog bed

- approaching a dog who is eating or chewing anything

- touching a dog who is being held on a lap or in someone's arms

- throwing things at or in the direction of the dog

- anything that you wouldn't permit your child to do to another child

- anything that elicits warning signs of stress in the dog.

TV and the movies

If you and your child see an ad, a TV program, or a movie that features a dog, talk with your child about which behavior depicted was safe and which was unsafe.

Think of it this way: How many times would you tolerate inappropriate touch from someone? It is risky to expect a dog to tolerate these things over and over. There are countless stories of children and adults doing these things and then, one day, regretting it. It's usually a matter of well-meaning people not knowing the correct way to interact with a dog. Here are just a few of the stories I know of first-hand:

- A professional dog walker walked the same dog daily for years. One day she greeted the dog as she had on other occasions. She bent over, talked sweetly to the dog, and, on this particular day, leaned over to kiss him on the head. He leapt up and bit her in the face. The injury required plastic surgery. Was this is a fluke? No. Visit any dog bite prevention website and ask any knowledgeable dog trainer, and they will tell you that human signs of affection, like hugging and kissing, are threatening to most dogs. It is up to us humans to refrain from initiating these well-meaning but threatening gestures.

- At a recent child-dog safety seminar I facilitated at a hospital, I had talked about hugs being threatening gestures to dogs, and how children must be taught not to hug dogs, both for the child's safety and the dog's well-being. After the presentation, an expectant mother approached me. The woman said she had a comment about the "no hugging" rule. I thought, "I bet she is going to tell me she doesn't like that rule." (Who could have blamed her? After all, it seems like such a natural thing to us humans, and of course we want to show dogs we love them.) But the woman did not object to the rule. Instead, she told me that she used to hug her dog all the time. Then one day she hugged her dog and he bit her on the face. She pointed out the scar that ran from the corner of her upper lip up to her nose. Based on what she learned at the seminar, she believed the dog had been showing subtle warning signs that she had not been aware of until she was bitten.

- Recently I was told a story by a dog owner who has no children. The dog he owned was adopted by him from the animal shelter specifically because it was assumed there would be no children in his home environment. However, his three-year-old nephew came to visit for the weekend. The dog had met the child before and had always seemed gentle when meeting kids, but the toddler had never visited for so many consecutive days. Perhaps the dog was feeling stressed by having been approached so many times. At one point on this particular weekend, the dog was resting on his bed in the same room as the child. His father was in the room too, but not coaching the child. When the toddler made his way toward the dog, the dog growled, and although the father heard the growl, he did not recognize it as a warning that the child should not come any closer. The child continued toward the dog's bed, and the dog responded by leaping up, knocking the child over, and biting his face just above the eye.

The moral of the story

For parents who wish to keep their child safe, just being in the same room is not enough. Supervision is not enough. Children must be coached through all their interactions with dogs so that they learn the dos and don'ts. Dogs must be monitored to make sure they are feeling at ease and not giving any warning signs (you'll learn about these warning signs in the next section). You can help prevent injury to your child and his or her friends by learning accurate information about dog and human body language. Follow the dos and don'ts list and teach your child to follow it, too.

Aside from safety, there is another, equally important reason not to do these threatening things to a dog. Most parents want their children to be kind, respectful, and empathetic to others, including dogs. A dog is not a toy, a doll, or a plaything to be danced with, dressed up, or played make-believe with. Dogs are individuals, with personalities, emotions, and thoughts. It is not appropriate to do things to them that we know will cause them to feel unsafe, afraid, angry, or threatened. We should make an effort to interact with dogs in ways that put them at ease and strengthen trust between us. Our children depend on us to teach them how to respect the feelings of others. Teaching them how to empathize with their canine pal is an important step.

Warning Signs that Even Your Dog Might Bite

Many people say their dog "seems fine" when touched in some of the inappropriate ways listed in the dos and don'ts section. In fact, I have heard people brag to others, "Oh, he's just great. He'll let the kids do anything to him." They don't realize it, but they are describing a dog who has not yet growled or bitten, but who is very, very likely throwing out all kinds of warning signs of stress, and even warning that a bite event is near. The truth is that it is risky and unfair to expect a dog to tolerate incorrect touch indefinitely.

How many times would you tolerate inappropriate touch from someone before you objected or tried to retreat? If the person continued touching you inappropriately, how many more times would you tolerate it before you warned the person, escalated your warning, or acted in physical self-defense?

Dog bites rarely come out of the blue. Most dogs use subtle but clear body language to warn that they are uncomfortable and may bite. Even the most well-meaning people often don't know how to interact with dogs in a way that avoids causing stress, and they usually don't notice dogs' early warnings.

Learn to notice the early warning signs that your dog is uncomfortable. Here are some common dog body signals that indicate mounting stress and a potential bite event. Make sure you and your child comply with the dos and don'ts in the previous section, as doing so will prevent most dogs from feeling ill at ease. Seek professional help (ask your veterinarian for a referral) if you observe your dog exhibiting any of the following warning signs:

- avoiding your child
- leaving the room when your child enters, or when your child makes certain sounds or movements
- turning her head away during an interaction
- flicking her tongue during an interaction
- moving away, even just a step or two
- walking away with your child following behind (teach your child not to follow the dog)
- mouthing or using her teeth on clothes or body for any reason
- standing motionless, particularly if approached by anyone while eating or in possession of a toy

- showing the whites of her eyes repeatedly

- showing dilated pupils (such that pupils look reflective or glowing)

- making furtive glances

- showing a furrowed brow

- shallow panting with her lips drawn back (as opposed to with her tongue hanging out like when dogs pant to cool off)

- trying to shove her body between you and your child

- growling (at anyone, however briefly)

- snarling (silently lifting her lip to show her teeth)

- snapping

- nipping

- biting

- whipping her head around toward anyone's hands when touched

- mounting/humping behavior toward people

- cringing, cowering, or hiding in reaction to movements or sounds made by your child

- staring intently at your child and whining

- staring silently or staring and barking at your child

- pacing and whining and/or panting near your child or where your child sleeps

- yawning, lip-licking or stretching

- licking paws or scratching the neck before, during, or following an interaction. Out-of-context grooming behaviors can be indicative of canine stress, similar to when a person feels uneasy and bites their nails, fiddles with their hair, or chews their lip.

- anything else that doesn't seem quite right or worries you.

This dog is showing several signs of stress: dilated pupils, wide rounded eyes, whites of the eyes, tongue flick, and turning away from the person. Photo by author.

Signs of stress and other emotions in dogs have been identified by scientists and other observers for centuries (Darwin famously catalogued many of these). Many of the subtlest warning signs of dog stress were identified by the dog behavior expert Sue Sternberg in the last decade. She collected and viewed hundreds of hours of videotape of thousands of dogs until she identified the patterns and subtleties of their communication system. One thing she found was that, in many instances, right before a dog bites, he will show a pattern of freezing motionless (often a series of quick freezes) and repeatedly show the whites of his eyes. These are fleeting behaviors that most people, even many animal professionals, do not learn to recognize. These subtle behaviors are like a red flag that a dog is very tense and that a bite event may be near. Recognizing such signs can help us prevent a bite because they show us that the dog needs help to cope better with certain stressors.

Left: Signs of stress this dog is showing include walking away, wide rounded eyes, dilated pupils, shallow panting. Notice that the children are petting over top the dog's back and more than one child is petting at a time. Reprinted with permission of *The News & Observer* of Raleigh, North Carolina.

Below: Faced with the prospect of being hugged, this dog stiffens, faces away from the person, leans away from the person, and shows the whites of his eyes. Photo by author.

Right: This dog shows a relaxed expression. Below: However, when someone attempts to touch him on top of the head, he looks down, avoids looking at the person and pulls his ears stiffly halfway back.

Next Page, Top: The person keeps petting incorrectly, so the dog looks away. Imagine how the dog feels. Bottom: The person switches to petting under the chin and on the side of the face. Notice the effect it has: the dog turns back towards the person, makes gentle eye contact, and his ears even begin to come forward a bit. Photos by author.

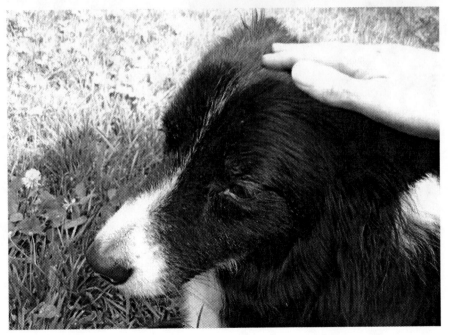

Happy Kids, Happy Dogs

Other Signs of Trouble

You may put your child and her playmates at risk if you chain or tie your dog outside. Dogs can become frustrated and behave in an aroused or aggressive manner if they are restrained in the presence of excited or playful children. If it is not a good time for your dog to be interacting with children, use the safety zone.

Other risk factors that you might see mentioned on the internet include the dog's level of training and his sterilization status. A couple of studies have shown that of dogs who had bitten, a significant number happened to be intact (not neutered) and had not attended dog obedience school. Please be aware that there could be a variety of reasons why those dogs showed up more often in the bite statistics than neutered dogs who were trained in a class. It could have been a statistical coincidence, a reflection of the general motivation level of the owner or the purpose for which the dog was acquired, or some other reason. It has not been proven that neutering your dog or taking him to obedience school will prevent or reduce the chances of him biting. There may be other reasons to neuter your dog or take a formal training class, but do not rely on these factors to keep your child safe.

You should be especially cautious if your dog tends to be aloof with people, even just with certain people. This personality trait usually means that the dog doesn't actively seek out much human contact, and if unsolicited touch is unwelcome to your dog, he may merely be tolerating it. To such a generally aloof dog, petting and touching is akin to your feelings when a salesperson in a store persistently insists on serving you when you were only trying to browse, causing you to eventually feel overwhelmed and irritated. One difference is that you can just leave the store, whereas, depending on the dog's personality, he may decide to use aggression to get the person to leave him alone. Note also that dogs who have an aloof personality often do not give a protracted series of warning signs as their stress and irritation builds, which means there is less time between the moment when the dog begins to feel annoyed and the moment when he bites. If you are not attuned to the subtle signs given by such a dog, the result may be a bite event that seems to have come "out of the blue."

Another sign that things are not well is if you find you are increasingly isolating your dog. If you find your dog is spending more and more time in the basement, out in the backyard, or tied up outside the house, it may be because something is wrong. Perhaps you are uneasy or unsure about your dog's behavior. Maybe he just seems a little out of control, or maybe you are having difficulty helping your child to feel at ease with your dog. If you notice this pattern of isolating the dog, please get professional help. It may indicate that the relationship is strained or that you sense it is risky to have your child and dog together. Your veterinarian can refer you to a qualified dog trainer or behavior consultant.

Learn to interpret dog body language

Here are some excellent resources to help you learn what your dog is communicating to you. They include many of the warning signs depicted in this section:

- *What Is My Dog Thinking?: The Essential Guide to Understanding Pet Behavior* by Gwen Bailey

- *Understanding Your Dog* by Bruce Fogle

- Body Language: What do you see? at http://www.diamondsintheruff.com/bodylang1.html. View each photo on this website and practice identifying the subtleties of dog body language depicted in each photo. Then drag your cursor over the photo to see a description and interpretation of the dog's body language.

- *Calming Signals: What Your Dog Tells You* by Turid Rugaas. I highly recommend this video, which shows many of the common signs of stress in dogs. The dog behavior footage is stellar. Different breeds and sizes are shown, so you can get practice recognizing the stress signals in various dogs. The video puts forth a hypothesis that we can mimic these signs to calm a dog down. Right now we don't know for sure if that is true (or even if dogs do that with each other), but one thing is for sure: I have yet to see another video that so accurately captures signs of dog stress.

How to Be an Effective Kid Canine Coach

In this section you will learn how to properly coach your child and dog through their interactions. The following instructions are organized according to your child's developmental stages. However, regardless of the child's age or behavior, always keep in mind the three principles for success outlined at the beginning of this chapter:

1. Meet your dog's daily needs for aerobic exercise, affection, and training.

2. Actively coach your child and dog through their interactions.

3. Use the safety zone when you are too tired or too busy to coach.

Infancy through crawling

I knew a family whose large dog did very well with their new baby. The dog maintained the good manners that her people had taught her. Even when the baby cried or needed a lot of attention from her people, the dog was relaxed and took it all in stride. Everything went very smoothly, at least at first. Then one day the parents took the baby with them on a two-week trip, and the dog stayed behind at a boarding facility. The evening after the family returned, they were all relaxing in the living room, as they had dozens of times before. The dog was lying on the floor near the sofa where the parents were seated. The baby began to crawl toward the sofa to get to her parents. A moment later, the dog leapt up and made a loud "Grrrrrowwfff!" sound as she lunged at the child's face, coming within an inch of making contact. The dog did not touch a hair on the child's head, but naturally the parents were quite alarmed. They were stunned that their dog would do such a thing. It seemed so out of the blue.

This story can teach us four important things. First, change can be very stressful for anyone. As humans, we generally understand what's going on when we make a change. Our dogs, however, can't understand or control a new situation. Consequently, they may find changes like trips (whether they come along or stay behind) to be quite taxing emotionally. The dog in this story may have been more stressed than usual. Whenever there is added stress in a dog's environment, whether from happy circumstances (guests, a new toy, a favorite person coming home) or from difficult circumstances (guests, a toenail trim, a trip, or a change in the baby) your dog may not behave as you've come to expect.

Second, dogs can be surprised by sudden developments. It just so happened that the baby in this story had learned to crawl during the two-week absence from the dog. The dog had no way of knowing that the child had suddenly become quite mobile and so she was taken by surprise, maybe even alarmed. It certainly seems as though she was trying to make the baby stop moving. It's important to gradually introduce your dog to the different things developing children do. That way there will be fewer surprises.

Third, you should not assume that just because you have a nice dog, she will be okay with your baby no matter what the baby does. The dog in this story was very gentle, mellow, well trained, and people-oriented. She had no problems with having valuable resources taken from her, and she enjoyed making new friends and being touched. She was relaxed if her people were sitting with the baby and never tried to cut off an interaction between them. This led her people to mistakenly assume that anything new the baby did would be okay with the dog, which is a very common mistake. It is imperative that you act proactively to prevent stress for your dog and potential injury to your baby. Assume change will be stressful for your dog and actively work to create pleasant associations with the baby as she grows and changes.

Finally, as I have stressed, supervision alone is not sufficient. The parents in this story were right there in the room, watching the child and the dog. The problem was, the parents did not actively coach them through the situation. Although the child and dog were close enough for either parent to touch within one second, that one second was not enough to stop the dog or to protect the baby. This story shows how incredibly fast, agile, and powerful dogs are. There is no way either parent would have been able to prevent a bite (or worse) to the baby, just by sitting close by and watching.

All of these lessons apply to your dog, too. Most importantly, note that supervision just doesn't cut it. You must be a what I call a kid canine coach. For infants that means doing several things.

Make sure your dog never has immediate access to the baby. Here's how to coach your dog and your baby during typical daily activities:

· Diaper change: Use a changing table so that the dog and baby are not down on the floor together, or put the dog in his safety zone for a moment. Use a diaper pail with a secure lid to prevent the dog from making a mess.

· Dog play time: Someone else seated on a piece of furniture should hold the baby in their lap, or put the baby in a car seat that is set up on a piece of furniture.

- Holding the baby: As long as the dog is relaxed and sitting, let the dog investigate the baby when the baby is in your arms or cradled in your lap (when you are seated on a piece of furniture). A tiny, relaxed dog can investigate by doing a "sit" or "down" calmly beside you on the furniture, but not on your lap or held in your other hand.

- Nursing or bottle-feeding the baby: If the dog is nearby he should sit or lie down at your feet, not beside you on the furniture. This goes for small dogs, too. You can also use the safety zone or hire a dog trainer to help you teach "go to your place" to direct your dog to lie down on a nearby mat.

- Multitasking during the baby's nap: If the baby is resting in a car seat, crib, or mechanical swing, your dog should be tethered with an edible chew toy, behind a baby gate, interacting with you, or in the safety zone. One client I knew would leave the infant in his car seat while she went to take a shower, but her dog was not confined and could go right up to the baby. Never do this. If you are fixing supper, talking on the phone, getting ready to go out, or doing some chore that requires you to pop in and out of the room, do not leave the child unattended for even a moment if the dog is not in her safety zone. The popular Baby Bjorn or other baby carrier that you wear might be a great help in such circumstances.

Actively help your dog develop pleasant associations with your baby, especially when your baby does something new.

Anytime there is a change, whether it is anticipated or sudden and unexpected, help your dog form a pleasant association with this "new version" of your baby. If the baby makes a new squeal, praise the dog and even feed him a treat. If the baby rolls over for the first time, gently pet the dog and use soothing tones. Keep treat canisters throughout the house so you'll have treats on hand when you need them. You want to help your dog make the association baby change = good!

Coach the crawl (or your baby's version of it!)

Whether your baby crawls, scoots on her butt, or goes straight to walking by holding your finger, you'll want your dog to think of this as the best thing ever. Enlist the aid of a helper, who will encourage your baby to crawl. You and your dog will observe this from behind a baby gate. Make sure your baby crawls toward the helper, who at first should be positioned away from you and your dog. Let your dog observe your baby crawling around. Gently praise and pet your dog while monitoring his behavior. If he is showing any signs of stress, create more distance between you and your baby and feed your dog high-value treats each time the dog looks at the baby. If the stress signs don't diminish at once, ask your vet for a referral to a qualified trainer.

Guide and encourage your crawling baby to move around the dog at angles, not straight at the dog. This is very easy. Your baby is probably heading for you, so position yourself such that he or she heads at an angle toward the dog. Praise your dog calmly and warmly when he looks at the baby. Occasionally toss a treat for your dog away from the direction your baby is crawling. If your crawling virtuoso is full of spunk and motoring around the room, the dog should be positioned behind a baby gate or in her safety zone so your baby cannot charge toward her.

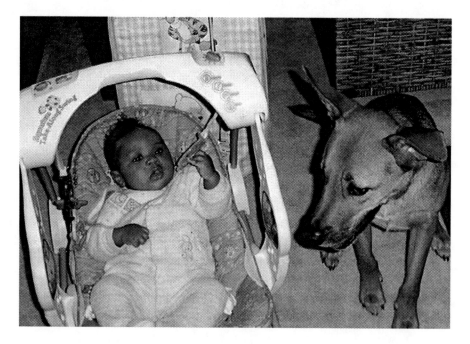

Don't put your vulnerable, uncoordinated child on the floor or couch with your dog, even for a photo. The parent who took this photo of their favorite family members did so without putting either one in harm's way. Photo courtesy of Jabrina Robinson.

Baby pictures with the dog

When you take pictures of your baby and dog together, have your baby seated on your lap and your dog seated on the floor beside you. Please don't put your baby and your dog together on the floor or bed and take their picture. Tiny babies need support to stay upright, so many well-meaning parents end up leaning their baby against the dog, which the dog is likely to find stressful or annoying. Is a picture really worth the risk of having your dog form an unpleasant association with your child? A better photo choice would be your baby sleeping in his bassinet with the dog seated or lying beside him. Crawling babies may sit with a toy in their hands (to prevent them grabbing at the dog with their strong little fists) while the dog is cued to sit beside them (provided, of course, the dog is not exhibiting any warning signs of stress).

Meal time

Has your dog figured out that hanging around the high chair at meal time has its advantages? If you don't want your dog cleaning up the morsels your baby drops, just put the dog in the safety zone with a food puzzle before meal time. Another idea is to ask your dog to lie down at the base of your baby's chair. His down-stay cue will thereby be reinforced with food treats each time your baby catapults something over the edge of the tray. This is a better solution than just letting your dog wander around and scavenge, which can distract your child from eating and encourage your dog to beg at the table.

When it comes to your dog's own meal time, be sure to feed him on schedule in his safety zone, so that he may eat undisturbed and so that his food bowl will not attract your child's attention. Dog food in your baby's mouth is not nearly as potentially harmful as the perception that your baby is honing in on your dog's feeding area (think back to the story in the introduction of this book). Keep fresh water available at all times, but position the bowl such that your child is less likely to encounter it. There's nothing quite like a baby splashing in the dog's water dish to help you remember this.

Preparing for the challenge of toddlerhood

Now is the time to make sure your dog develops plenty of happy associations with crawling, stumbling, and running children. Why? Because in a few weeks or months, your baby will be a crawling, stumbling, running child, who is friends with more of the same. Get together with friends who have children and visit parks and playgrounds *before* your own child reaches this stage. Get just close enough with your dog that she can perceive the sounds and movements of the kids. Ask her to sit and do some of her tricks. Feed her plenty of high-value treats. Practice for five or ten minutes, and then go home. Doing this a few times a week would be ideal.

If this goes well, next time bring along a friend who can supervise your baby while you work with your dog. If your dog is relaxed, and free of signs of stress, move closer to the playing children. It is likely that at least one child will show interest in your dog and move toward you. First, check in with the guardians of any interested children so they can coach them on how to correctly interact with the dog (see section on correctly meeting dogs in chapter 4). Next, be sure that the children pet the dog only one at a time, while you feed treats and warmly praise your dog. After a few moments, cheerfully say, "let's go," and turn away from the group with your dog to give her a break between kids and to monitor her for any signs of stress. If she is not completely relaxed, offer to show off some of her tricks instead of having the children come closer. If, at any point, you find that the children are too exuberant or not under the control of their guardians, cheerfully turn away with your dog and return another day.

Toddlerhood from the dog's perspective

What must our dogs think when our baby learns to stand and toddle around? Such a metamorphosis must be mind-blowing for the dog to behold. Here are some guidelines for making this transition go smoothly.

This dog is learning to feel calm and happy about the little girl learning to walk. When the dog notices an awkward movement by the child, he is fed a treat.
Photo by Christopher Sims.

Toddler movement

Any time your dog notices your toddler, calmly praise him and, when possible, reward him with food treats. To a dog, nearly all toddler movements may seem strange, annoying, or even frightening. When your toddler attempts to walk, staggers around, or then plops down on his butt or face, your dog may cock his head as if to say, "Oh my goodness, I don't know what happened to the baby, but what is that thing?" When your dog notices your toddler, use praise and gentle petting, as well as occasional treats when you can, in order to reinforce that idea that toddler = good!

Teaching how to pet the dog

Very young children can't pet a dog with smooth, gentle movements. Heck, they can't even hold their fingers and palms out flat. They just don't yet have that kind of motor control. They're much more likely to flail their arms up and down, and to grasp things rather than gently touch them. This is just the reality of child development. However, your dog is not a punching bag. We have to look out for him; otherwise he may wonder why the toddler treats him so poorly.

Lisa is teaching little Zoe the correct way to show affection to their dog Mattie. Mom lets Zoe watch first. Photo by author.

Luckily, you can show your child what to do by using a plush toy dog to start. Let her watch you pet the toy dog with your hand, then let her hand go along for the ride on the back of yours. Gradually guide her hand in the correct motion. In soothing tones, repeat "Gentle, gentle," to help her feel good about the experience. This also gives this special kind of touch a name so it will transfer more easily to your dog. A few strokes are fine. Calmly end the session before she wants to grab onto the toy's "fur."

When your toddler is in a quiet, calm mood (or as close as she comes to that), transfer your "gentle" lesson to the dog. Keep it short and successful. Your child may sit on your lap with your dog sitting near you, or she may stand on the floor, facing roughly the same direction as the dog (not face to face with the dog) with the dog sitting or standing. Lying down is not as good a position for your dog, because it teaches your child that it's okay to approach a dog who's resting (which it isn't). Besides, we want to give the dog an easy position from which he can leave if he feels uncomfortable. Praise your dog warmly and feed him treats during the interaction. Before it is too much for either child or dog (refer to the dog stress warning signs section), pick your child up and redirect her to some other activity.

Then Lisa coaches Zoe how to pet Mattie on the chest. Photo by author.

Happy Kids, Happy Dogs

Be aware that if you try to prevent your toddler from touching the dog altogether, it may cause her to become fascinated with the dog and obsessed with touching him. This can contribute to her harassing the dog at some point. We also don't want to put her in a situation in which you need to tell her "no!" and "don't!" a lot. Besides being stressful for you, so many verbal reprimands may lead your child and your dog to form an unpleasant association with each other. It's better to practice planned interactions that are gentle and successful. If your toddler is not quite ready to touch your dog, point out the dog's ears, eyes and nose while naming them, all the while feeding your dog some treats.

Toddler behaviors to prevent

Do not allow your toddler to lean on your dog, use him to help her stand up or maintain her balance, grasp or pull at his fur or any body parts, or make a beeline for the dog (either slowly or quickly). Give your child lots of praise and encouragement during your frequent gentle petting sessions, so that he or she won't be tempted to try threatening gestures like hugging or kissing the dog. If any of these should somehow occur before you can redirect your child, quickly cue your dog to come to you, or use your "touch" cue if you are close together.

As your child grows, she will develop all kinds of new and amazing physical and mental skills. While we humans may delight in these ("Why, look! Little Henrietta is flinging kitchen utensils all over the floor!"), some of these new behaviors will be quite startling, frightening, or annoying to your dog. Monitor your dog to note how he deals with your child screeching, stumbling, crying, and throwing things. Lavish special praise and treats on your dog when these occur. ("What a good dog! I'm so proud of you. Would you like a break?") Prevent too much stressful exposure to your child by occupying your dog with food puzzles in the safety zone rather than insisting he be around the child

A note about germs

The best thing you can do to prevent your child from contracting parasites from your dog is to follow your veterinarian's prevention recommendations for hookworm, roundworm, fleas, and ticks. Keep your yard free of dog feces. Your dog is probably going to lick your child, which is unlikely to cause harm. Besides, you might go a little loopy if you attempt to clean your child's hands every time she interacts with the dog. Save your energy for kid canine coaching!

all the time. Use the dos and don'ts list earlier in this chapter as a guide to encourage correct behavior from your child. Continue to meet your dog's daily needs for physical and mental exercise so that you may use the safety zone whenever you need to, without feeling guilty. This will spare you from constantly having to protect your dog from your child, and your child from your dog.

The terrible twos through age four

If you have a child aged four or younger and you don't yet have a dog but are considering getting one (or are considering getting another dog), don't do it. Every client I have ever had who has done this would beg you to reconsider. One client of mine, the mother of a three-year-old girl, spoke with her vet before purchasing a puppy. The vet advised against getting a dog because of her daughter's age. He tried to explain how much effort it would be to manage, teach, and coach the dog and child, both separately and together. The mother protested, saying that her daughter was an especially mature three year old (which was true). Some time later, as she relayed this conversation to me, she looked down at the dog and her daughter, and then rolled her eyes in exasperation as if to say, "Good grief, what was I thinking?!" If you don't yet have a dog, or you are considering adding another dog to your family, age five is the youngest I would recommend embarking on this fun but exhausting journey. For more information, see the section on how to choose the right dog for your family in chapter 4.

If your child is between the ages of two and four and you already have a dog, it is very important for you to act as an effective kid canine coach. Kid canine coaching at this age means showing your child what to do each time he or she is in the dog's presence. Refer to the dos and don'ts list in the last section. Monitor your dog's warning signs. If you see any, err on the side of caution and ask your vet for a referral to a qualified trainer or behavior consultant who can work with you, your dog, and your child. Do not wait until the warning signs build up and escalate to a growl or a bite. Take the warning signs seriously and get qualified, professional help. Your child must also learn to never, ever disturb the dog in the safety zone. Explain that the dog is having nap time there and must never be spoken to or stared at in his "room."

Ages two through four is the time when children can really begin to interact with their dogs. With the proper guidance from you, a gentle relationship can start to grow. Many of the things on the dos list are appropriate for this age range. Quiet singing to the dog can be a soothing activity. Giving kisses by kissing hands and petting the dog is also a favorite of younger children. Even a very young child can help pour the dog's kibble into a doggie food puzzle. One of my clients has a two-year-old daughter who commands their dog to sit, in totally incomprehensible English. The dog's eyebrows twitch as he

When Zoe reaches over Mattie's head, she turns away. That's stressful for the dog. (It would also be better if Mattie was in a "sit" position, but she flopped into a down on her own during the session.) Photo by author.

translates in his mind, then he sits, and she feeds him a treat. It is one of the cutest things I've ever seen. And it signals the beginning of a beautiful friendship.

As your child grows older and more coordinated and he is ready to start helping with simple household chores, he may assist you with many doggie chores as well. He can help you rotate the toys in the safety zone (but only when the dog is not actually in the safety zone), give the dog a meal or fresh water, and be in charge of carrying (clean) doggie clean-up bags on walks. Some three- and four-year-old children may even like to do tricks with the dog and feed them treats as a reward. Younger children can watch you cue the trick, then they can be in charge of feeding your dog a treat as a reward.

Ages five through twelve

Continue to coach your dog and child whenever they are together. Reward your child for complying with the dos and don'ts. Monitor your dog for warning signs. Use the safety zone if you cannot provide a coaching session. If that seems like a lot of work, consider that children ages five through nine are the people at highest risk for dog bites—and remember, it is most often the family dog or a friend's dog doing the biting.

Lisa reminds Zoe the correct way to touch the dog. Mattie looks much more relaxed and has turned toward them again. Notice that Lisa's hand is guiding Zoe's, and that she is smiling and praising both Zoe and Mattie. Photo by author.

Teach and demonstrate the dos and don'ts so that your child will be safer around your dog and other dogs outside your home. Don't leave your child alone with your dog any more than you would leave her unattended with knives, a ladder, or a stove.

How to feed a treat

Children should feed dog treats with the treat resting on the flat of their palm, thumb held tight with the side of the hand. They (or you) can say, "get it," to the dog as they move their flat palm towards the dog. This way the dog has verbal permission as well as a visual cue to take the treat, and will be less likely to grab unauthorized goodies from your child at other times.

Above: Here daughter Zoe shows she is uncomfortable with great big Mattie approaching her. To prevent Mattie the dog from invading Zoe's space, Lisa intervenes by saying, "Mattie, touch!"

Right: Which cues Mattie to bop the palm of Lisa's hand with her nose. (See chapter 1 for how to teach this.) Photos by author.

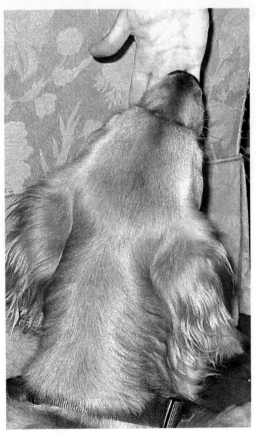

Top: Zoe is now more comfortable and has moved closer to her mom. Lisa cues "touch" again to move Mattie even further from Zoe.

Bottom: Zoe is now so at ease that she decides to feed Mattie a treat. A very nice example of kid canine coaching by mom! Photos by author.

This youngster is learning to feed the dog his supper.
Photo courtesy of Celeste Huntington.

At this age your child may play fetch with your dog under your supervision, take on more of the doggie chores with your help, and use his imagination to teach special tricks as you watch. I always love having families in dog-training class with children this age. They usually make wonderful trainers, seem to empathize with their dogs, and often make the most hilarious observations. Consider taking a group dog-training class with your child. This will also help you instill in him the proper procedures for meeting other dogs.

You may be tempted to let your older child take your dog for walks without you. Believe it or not, this is a very bad idea. For one thing, it means sending your child to wander around the neighborhood or park without adult supervision. Your dog is not Lassie, Wishbone or Winn Dixie. Those were actors, and in real life would not have been allowed by responsible adults to go on a walk with an unsupervised child. Another safety consideration involves size. Picture your child hanging onto the end of the leash the moment your dog glimpses a squirrel or a cat to chase. I've seen confident, good-sized seven-year-olds get the daylights scared out of them in that situation, dropping the leash in desperation. It would be horrible if your child were injured, lost your dog or witnessed her being hit by a car because he couldn't hang on.

Notice the dog automatically "says please" by sitting. He will not go to his dish until he is given permission to get up from the sit with the verbal cue "okay."
Photo courtesy of Celeste Huntington.

The most important thing to realize is that a child this age is not old enough to cope with the many decisions that need to be made on an average walk, such as which dogs are okay for your dog to meet, what to do if your dog jumps on someone, or how to handle it if your dog shows aggressive behavior toward others. I had a client whose dog behaved with uncertainty around strangers. I recommended she never allow her ten-year-old son to walk the dog alone and explained to her what could happen, but she allowed it anyway. One day, her son and their dog passed a stranger. The dog lunged and bit the person, who then called the police. When the police came, they took the dog to be quarantined. How do you suppose that made the little boy feel? How do you suppose the mother felt? And that's not to mention the lawsuit she could have had on her hands. Please don't put your child, yourself, and your dog in this position. Instead, teach your child to play fetch in the yard while you coach them, or enjoy a walk together with the dog. This is also a great time to hear about your child's school day while you get some fresh air together. Think of it as a tradition that you can begin with your child that will last throughout his or her pre-teen years.

Happy Kids, Happy Dogs

A walk with your child and your dog is a nice way to spend quality time together, and helps give everyone some exercise. This dad, equipped with poop bags and a treat pouch, holds the leash in one hand and his daughter's hand in the other.
Photo courtesy of
Celeste Huntington.

A boy and a puppy enjoy a quiet moment together.
Photo courtesy of Kirstin Lawler.

Your dog and your teenager

There are three important things to be aware of when it comes to dogs and teenagers:

1. You can count on your teenager developing interests that have nothing to do with your dog. It may be challenging to get your budding adult to complete daily chores or to follow through on dog-related commitments.

2. Teenagers, and even younger kids, sometimes confide in a dog during turbulent times. This can be a nice bridge to conversations with you. Consider taking a hike, a walk through the neighborhood, or another outing together as a way to reconnect with each other.

3. Finally, and unfortunately, teenagers are most often the juvenile perpetrators of cruelty toward domestic animals (read more about this in a later section). For kid canine coaching purposes, note that harmful acts toward dogs by kids usually happen clandestinely, so watch your teenager and your dog. Be at home when he or she has friends over, so that you can monitor behavior toward your dog by your child and his guests and notice any dog warning signs. Always demonstrate the dos and don'ts to help your child develops empathy and respect for your dog and other creatures.

Remember: Supervision just doesn't cut it

I hear people say all the time, "I supervise my child and dog. As long as I know where they are and can keep an eye on them, they are fine." While "keeping an eye on them" is a good rule of thumb for humans of a certain age, it is never a sufficient rule of thumb for the very special combination of children and dogs.

You may be able to make supper while your infant snoozes in his car seat. Or perhaps your four-year-old child plays with toys in the back yard while you glance occasionally out the kitchen window. This is fine supervision for kids who don't have a dog in their family. It is not fine for kids with dogs. If "keeping an eye on them" is your idea of supervising your child and dog, then I'm afraid you are putting them both at risk.

There are two appropriate places for children and dogs to be in your household:

1. Together under the direction of a kid canine coach, meaning that you are actively teaching your child the correct way to behave around your dog, and you are actively monitoring your dog's body language for any signs of stress (of course, with you heartily rewarding both of them for appropriate behavior).

2. If you don't have time or energy for a coaching session, or if you just need to step out of the room for a moment, then your dog should be confined in his safety zone where he is not to be disturbed, or else your child should be tucked in his room (with the door closed) out of reach of the dog.

With a knowledgeable kid canine coach guiding their interactions, your child and your dog can look forward to a solid relationship and years of happy times together.

Young but Not Foolish:
Games Kids Can Play with Their Dogs

There are many benefits to children and dogs playing the right kinds of games together. Games are a way for your child and dog to bond. Games are a way for them to learn about rules, fairness, and patience. Games can help your dog maintain a positive association with your child. They help tire kids and dogs out (talk about a benefit everyone can enjoy!). And, of course, games are just plain fun.

Find it

Object: for your dog to use only his nose to find treats that you and your child have hidden.

This game challenges your dog's natural senses and problem-solving abilities. The more he does this in an appropriate context, the less he'll seek out inappropriate outlets (like the counter, the trash, the plant in the living room).

Hold your dog by the collar. Have your child show the dog a tasty tidbit and then dramatically place it on the ground about three feet away. When your child cues "find it," release the dog and watch the dog devour the treat. Do this three times in quick succession.

Next, hide the treat about the same distance away, but obscure it with another object, like the leg of a coffee table. Repeat the same process of holding the collar, hiding the treat, saying "find it!," and then releasing the dog.

To tug or not to tug

Tug-of-war is one of my favorite games to play with a dog. However, because of the sheer strength and good judgment needed to play safely, I don't recommend it for children. Even teenagers tend to get too wound up to make tug a good idea. Save it for grown-ups, when the children are at school or otherwise out of sight. Teach a reliable "drop it" cue, and use only a special tug toy that you put away afterward.

Once your dog is rushing over and easily finding the treat right away, start adding difficulty. Your child should bend as though he is dropping the treat, but shouldn't actually place it in the familiar spot. Instead, he'll place it in a new location close by, like behind the other coffee table leg or the magazine rack. When your child says "find it," your dog will have to hunt around a bit with his nose. He won't be sure where the real treat is, since you have created a decoy treat placement. Practice a few times in a row, then end the session. Once your child and your dog master this, hide the treat in the next room, out in the open. If your dog finds it with no trouble, start hiding the treats in the next room, behind the door or a piece of furniture.

Gradually increase the level of difficulty until your dog has to hunt for several minutes, searching all over the house for his treats or even his dinner. You can chat on the phone, pay the bills, nurse the baby, or eat dinner in peace while meeting your dog's mental exercise requirements! Try hiding multiple treats, so he is intermittently rewarded as he goes. If the weather is poor and you can't exercise your dog outside as much, you'll be glad he's got something to do inside that is challenging for his mind and body. On nice days, try this outdoors. He could hunt down his whole breakfast while you get the kids ready for school, vacuum the house, or check your e-mail. Everyone wins!

Find me

Object: for your dog to find your child on cue.

This is a great game that teaches your dog to pay attention to your child both inside and outside. Plus, it's very interactive without involving running and shouting. Start indoors and plan to hide behind a chair in the same room as your dog. A helper (who could be your child if he or she is large enough to not be pulled over by the dog) should hold the dog while you sneak off and hide. I recommend being very dramatic about this by crouching on tip-toe and glancing back at the dog as you sneak away and hide. This will really pique your dog's interest. Then say, "find me!" When your dog does find you, lavish praise and treats on him. Make it obvious where you are hiding at first until he gets the idea. Then get your child in on the game. Hold your dog while your child hides behind the chair and calls, "find me!" Very slow, exaggerated sneaking off is one of the best parts of this game, so your child should play it up!

Once your dog has gotten the hang of this, have your child try hiding in another room, then in another room behind a door. Show your child how to offer lots of praise and treats each time your dog finds him. A variation on this game is to quietly ask your dog to find your son or daughter by name, for example, "Where's Johnny?" as you hold him back by the collar, waiting for your child to call out. Then your dog will associate the phrase, "Where's Johnny?" with the urge to go find your child.

Getting a head start

If you need to help your child to hide and therefore can't hold your dog by the collar, toss a treat away from you, past the dog, to get a head start before you call out "find me." This will give your dog time to count to ten, so to speak.

Gradually increase the level of difficulty by playing "find me" even when there are distractions, like other people in the house, animal noises on TV, or someone preparing dinner. For the best workout, try it outdoors in safe, fenced-in locations. Once you move it to such a challenging location, reward your dog with real meat treats.

Two-toy fetch

Object: for your dog to bring back the toy your child throws, and drop it at his feet, so that your child will throw the second ball.

Fetch is a great game of cooperation that helps meet the dog's daily need for exercise.
Photo by Christopher Sims.

I first read about a version of this in a book by the dog trainer Sheila Booth. I recommend this as the preferred method for a child and dog to play fetch, since it is based on your child always having control of one ball, and your dog willingly and automatically offering the other ball. It eliminates the need for anyone to reach for the dog when he is in possession of a toy.

Teach this to your dog first, then show your child how to do it. This is a great method for dogs who go after the ball but don't bring it back, dogs who bring it halfway back, or dogs who would rather tug with the toy than give it up once they do bring it back. It's a great game for kids and dogs because it's all about sharing, not grabbing.

- Pick an area in which to play. Indoors in a hallway is a good place to start (fewer distractions means a greater chance for success).

- Choose two of the exact same toys (they must be identical).

- Be excited about the two toys you have. Act silly and giggle a little.

- Toss the first toy about ten feet and silently watch as your dog goes after it.

- When she grabs it in her mouth, take off running, still silently, in the opposite direction from her. She will likely chase you.

- Don't look back to see if she's coming, look where you're going or it won't work (and you may trip and fall down).

- When you can hear your dog catch up to you, slow to a stop and begin making a huge fuss over the second toy, which is still in your hand. Toss it up in the air and catch it, sniff it, talk goofy to it.

- Do not talk to or look at your dog, do not call her name or encourage her. You are way too busy with this fabulous second toy to have any time for that. We are talking Olympic-level keep-away here.

- If your dog moves away from you, run away from her hooting about how great the second toy is.

- Most dogs cannot resist this, and, sometimes instantly, sometimes after a couple of minutes, will rush up to you. They are convinced the toy in your hands must be better than the one they have (otherwise, why all the fuss?). At this point, your dog will drop the toy in her mouth.

- This next part is crucial. The very instant she drops her toy on the ground, you must immediately say, "good!" and throw the second toy, underhand like a bowling ball. You have to be fast and enthusiastic about telling her "good!" and then releasing the other toy. We want her to understand that racing back to you and dropping her toy at your feet is what immediately gets her the amazing, much-coveted, clearly better second toy.

- Remember to throw underhand, aiming for the ground near where you're standing so that she'll be able to see the toy leave your hand.

- At this point, and no sooner, you may pick up the toy that she has dropped. She's already far away, chasing the toy you've just thrown. Get ready to start the cycle all over!

- It is important to stop playing *before* your dog gets too tired or bored, so that she will be enthusiastic about playing again next time.

Kids about age six and older can play this game with you coaching. As with all good things your dog gets, have her sit before starting the game. Once you start the game, just keep going without having her sit for each throw. If she should get too wound up, just freeze and act like a mannequin and wait for a sit before tossing the toy again.

Ricochet recall

Object: to get your dog running enthusiastically from family member to family member when called.

Two or three family members stand about thirty feet apart, all holding special treats. Take turns saying, "Fifi, come!" then cheering wildly. If your dog hesitates *even for a moment*, take off cheering in the opposite direction and she should come bounding after you. Feed her favorite treats when she reaches you. To get her to "ricochet" to the next family member, withdraw your attention and the treats momentarily while the next person cheers and calls her over to them. Repeat this two or three times, stopping before the dog gets bored.

Tricks

Object: to have your dog perform a novel, fun, mind-challenging behavior on cue.

Tricks help your child and your dog because they:

- · are fun to teach and show off

- · help your nervous dog or child calm down

- · give your energetic dog or child something to focus on

- · show you how your dog learns so you can teach her just about anything

- · increase your dog's responsiveness to your child.

To teach a trick, use one of the following strategies:

- · *Lure* your dog with a treat into the behavior or position you like, then say "yes" and feed him a treat. For example, for "roll over," begin with your dog in the down position. He should follow a treat in your hand until he flops over; then say "yes" and feed him a treat.

- · *Shape* a behavior your dog offers by saying "yes" and rewarding him in tiny increments toward the finished product. For example, at first you say "yes" and feed your dog a treat for merely going near a mat. Then you withhold the treat for going near it and wait for a new behavior, such as sniffing the mat. You say "yes" and reward for sniffing the mat, then for accidentally stepping or sitting on it. Once your dog consistently sits on the mat, you then withhold treats for the sit behavior and wait for a new behavior. Your dog may leave, or yawn, or jump, but you will ignore these behaviors and say "yes" and reward only for lying down. Eventually your dog will put all the parts together and go to the mat and lie down in one fluid movement.

Teaching tricks is good for mental exercise and relationship-building, as well being fun for both child and dog. Photo by author.

- *Capture* a cute behavior your dog already does on his own by saying "yes" and rewarding him when he does it, or just applying the cue word to his behavior. For example, your dog stretches after a nap and you say "take a bow!" each time, just as he's about to stretch.

Except for capturing, it doesn't make much sense to apply the cue word to your trick until you have the final, polished version. After all, you don't want to say "roll over" and have your dog associate that with going only halfway over. So save adding the cue word until your dog has the idea. She doesn't speak English anyway, so the words won't help her learn it. Think of the cue word, or command, as being the finishing touch once you're happy with the trick.

Troubleshooting tricks:
If things aren't going as smoothly as you'd like, ask yourself:

- Is the environment too distracting for the dog or the child?

- Are my treats sufficiently exciting to my dog?

Happy Kids, Happy Dogs

- Am I breaking the trick up into small enough pieces for the dog and the child to master at one time?

- Am I giving sufficient rewards?

- Am I keeping the training sessions short (around five minutes) and ending on a high note?

- Where is my hand that's holding the treat? Am I holding it low enough or high enough to help the dog's body get into position?

The following are some of my clients' favorites tricks:

- spin (dog does a little pirouette in front of you, all four paws on the floor)

- high five

- go night-night (dog lies motionless on her side)

- catch (dog catches a ball or treat in his mouth)

- shake

- roll over

- crawl

- take a bow.

The easiest way to get started is just to "lure" your dog with a treat into the behavior or position you like, then feed him a treat. There are great books and videos available that explain all the steps to teach your dog these tricks. Check out the appendix for suggestions. It's easy and it's fun!

Besides tricks, your child and your dog may also enjoy these two activities:

Hula Dog

Object: to have the dog negotiate obstacles on cue, giving your dog and child a chance to be active together, but in a controlled way.

To play hula dog, all you need is a regular hula hoop from a toy store. First let your dog explore the hula hoop when it's lying still on the ground. Encourage your dog to explore by tapping the hoop with your hand and praising. Then have your child walk over the hula hoop a few times, feeding your dog treats for following her and stepping over the edges of the hoop. Next, tilt the hoop up and hold it steady so that it is balancing on edge on the ground. Encourage your dog to sniff the hoop to earn a treat. As you hold the hoop, stand aside so there is nothing blocking its opening. Your child should crouch and step through it, leaving your dog on one side of the hoop. Then your child may show the dog a treat. If your dog cranes his neck forward and pokes it through the hoop, your child may feed him the treat. Keep offering and feeding treats for small successes, until the dog passes through the hoop in one smooth movement. Your child will need to back up bit by bit from the hoop as your dog becomes more proficient (eventually moving back a couple of feet depending on the size of your dog).

Finally, raise the hoop about one inch off the ground. Make sure your child is standing on the other side of the hoop as usual, with a couple of feet between her and the hoop. If your dog hops though, your child may praise him and feed him a treat. If your dog hesitates, try raising the hoop only half an inch at first. Once your dog hops through easily, you can add the cue, "hula!" just before he hops through.

You can expand hula dog into a homemade obstacle course in your yard. (Playing indoors on a rainy day can work, too.) Your doggie obstacle course could include:

- a broomstick, positioned horizontally and propped up with a paperback book on each end (to make a mini-hurdle)

- a kiddie pool (filled with water or empty)

- a colorful beach towel where a sit-stay can be performed (for five to fifteen seconds)

- a beach chair or beach ball, for leading the dog by the leash around in a little circle (for variety use two chairs and walk with the dog in a figure 8 pattern around them)

- sofa cushions or a sheet propped up to form a tunnel to crawl through.

Sit then spaz out

Object: to get the dog to sit instantly, even if she is really wound up. I had a client whose son played very roughly with their dog. He would tackle the dog, chase the dog and catch him tightly, and even ambush the dog. Naturally the dog started avoiding the child and biting him if he couldn't get away in time. Even though the dog was actually a very normal, even-tempered dog, this pattern became a big problem and could have led to injuries and the dog being given up.

First we had to teach the child how his rough behavior made the dog feel vulnerable, afraid, and defensive. The child honestly didn't know, since that's how the boy played with his human friends sometimes, and that's how the dog seemed to play with the neighbor's dog. Then we taught the child to play "sit then spaz out" with his dog. He was a very smart, athletic child, so he caught on quickly and the dog was delighted to play an appropriate, safe, fun game. It's a very active game that is great for teaching self-control.

To play the game, the child holds two handfuls of treats. The game starts with a sit ("say please"), then the child feeds her a treat. He then says, "spaz!" and zooms off in a sprint. As the dog catches up, the child turns to face the dog and says, "sit." When the dog complies, she is fed a treat. The treat should be fed low to prevent jumping up. Then the sequence starts again. For fun and skill, the child should vary how long the dog must hold the sit before another spaz is announced. Quick changes of direction are nice for variety, as is varying the length of each sprint. For best results, first teach this to the dog without the child present, so she'll already have the idea, then show your child and let them try. This game does not involve screaming, waving arms around, falling down, or any other out-of-control behavior. Of course, it should always be played with a kid canine coach guiding the action.

When Other Kids Visit

A client came to see me with her large dog. She was worried because he had growled and snapped at a visiting child. She was very concerned, not only because of her dog's size, but for her own son's safety. She told me that two girls, ages five and seven, had come for a visit with their mother. The owner and her dog met them out in the carport. The girls were a bit wound up and were waving toys in the dog's face. After a while, the dog went into the house, probably to get some relief from the commotion, but the girls followed him. The mothers stayed outside. Inside the house, the dog continued to move away from the girls, but they continued to follow him. Eventually the dog ran out of space and found himself in the corner of a room. The girls continued to approach him, and one of them reached for the dog, who responded by growling. When the girl continued to reach the dog snapped at her. Although he didn't make contact with her, the girls then recognized the dog was not feeling friendly, so they went and told the adults.

There are several very important lessons to be learned from this story, which is repeated frequently in households all over the country.

Lesson 1: Parental supervision is not sufficient to prevent problems between children and dogs. The girls' mothers were right there, but they did not coach the kids in the correct behavior, nor did they monitor the dog for warning signs. The shouting and waving toys in the dog's face were inappropriate. The dog turning and leaving was a red flag that went unnoticed. A kid canine coach notices these things and then gives the child instructions for better behavior, and helps the dog to the peace and quiet of his safety zone.

When a dog walks away, a child must not follow. When dogs are stressed they sometimes leave to avoid a confrontation. By following a dog who is trying to retreat, the child can make the dog feel threatened. Threatened dogs sometimes bite.

The children were left alone with the dog. It only takes a few moments for things to escalate. Not minutes, moments. It is not okay to leave a dog and a child unattended, ever, even just to get a drink of water, a baby wipe, to finish a conversation, or to pick up the phone. Without a kid canine coach present, children have been injured and even killed in a matter of seconds. Don't put your child or your dog in this position.

Lesson 2: The girls went to get an adult, which was a great idea. Kids should not interact with a dog without a kid canine coach helping them out. It was terrific that the girls recognized the dog's escalating signs of stress and went to get an adult.

Lesson 3: Be aware of extra stress in your dog's life. Stress just means a change in your dog's environment that can affect his behavior. It can be happy stress or bad stress, but either way it may result in your dog having trouble coping. The extra stress in the above situation came from visitors arriving and from the girls' inappropriate behavior. Furthermore, the dog had been feeling discomfort recently. The veterinarian had been called to examine the dog, and the exam had occurred in the carport. The dog had also been acting nervously outside recently due to the installation of an electric shock fence. All of this may have contributed to the dog feeling threatened. A dog who feels stressed may feel he needs to act in self-defense. Depending on the dog and the situation, self-defense may mean retreating, giving warning signs, or even biting. When there is extra stress in your dog's environment, err on the side of caution and use the safety zone to give him some down time.

Lesson 4: The dog in the above anecdote had had many previous happy encounters with these girls in the past. Just because the visitors know your dog, does not mean you can ease off your kid canine coaching. In fact, it's just the opposite. Children are likely to be less inhibited with a familiar dog, which means they might do inappropriate things to the dog, who will in turn feel threatened and possibly bite. Just because your dog knows a certain child does not make it okay to leave your dog to his own defense or put the child at risk. Each encounter requires coaching. Each encounter will either help the children and the dog respect and enjoy each other more, or it will make them more likely to have trouble on the next encounter.

Rules to follow when kids visit your home

When children visit your home there are several things you should do:

First, teach them how to pet your dog. Children may pet one at a time. They may pet under the chin or on the chest. They should use an "inside voice" around the dog. If any child breaks a rule, the dog gets to enjoy a toy in her safety zone. The kids must never disturb the dog in the safety zone.

Monitor the dog for signs of stress, and use the safety zone all or part of the time. If you notice your dog start to exhibit warning signs, bring her to her safety zone. Better yet, if it's clear the kids are starting to get excited, put your dog in the safety zone before she starts to display warning signs.

Consider the children who are coming over to visit. How many will there be? Will their parent or guardian be there to monitor their behavior? Are they generally reserved or more on the precocious side? Do they have a dog at home? If so, this could make for riskier behavior around your dog. The child may try inappropriate things with your dog that he has perhaps rehearsed at home with his own dog. On the other hand, if the child does not have a dog at home, it could make him more fearful of or more curious about your dog. In other words, either way, the child will need you to act as kid canine coach.

Nikki the dog is learning a positive association with Judy's grandson, who in turn is learning safe, respectful behavior around dogs. These two will be fast friends in no time.
Photo courtesy of Judy and Doug Schill.

In the photo on this page we see Judy teaching her visiting grandson to offer her dog Nikki a treat. Notice how loose the leash is. There is no need for tension on the leash because Nikki has been taught to "say please" by sitting in exchange for good things. Judy is positioned so that she can guide the little boy's hand if necessary. Notice that Judy's eyes are on the dog, monitoring for signs of stress, while she instructs her grandson. This is kid canine coaching at its finest.

I once got a phone call from someone who said her dog had started bolting after children, running, growling, and barking at them on sight. The dog had always been placid around kids, until the day a child visited her, became curious, and shoved a pencil into the dog's ear. The pencil-poking child was lucky she was not bitten in the face that day. Now there is another dog out there who is convinced that children are unpredictable and dangerous. She now threatens them on sight.

Happy Kids, Happy Dogs

Please, if you have child visitors over, place your dog in his safety zone. With gentle children who will follow instructions, you may allow interactions, but always be a kid canine coach, monitoring your dog for warning signs. If you do see any warning signs, don't make excuses or rationalizations, cheerfully remove the dog to his safety zone before continuing the visit. These simple guidelines will help keep your young visitors safer and teach them good habits. They will also help keep your dog feeling at ease with children, so that at subsequent visits he associates them with feeling safe.

What Parents Need To Know About Violence Toward Companion Animals

This section is not just for the parents down the street or across town. It is for you and your family. Cruelty or abuse toward animals is more common than you might imagine, and can start as early as late toddlerhood, emerge during the teenage years, or be perpetrated by adults. There is no one universal definition, but animal abuse usually refers to inappropriate behavior intended to cause harm, distress, pain, suffering, or death. You should be concerned if your child shows abusive or cruel behavior toward your dog or other creatures. There is a correlation between domestic violence and other forms of violence and animal abuse. The presence of one may indicate another is also occurring.

- Domestic violence has been linked to animal abuse. Abused women in safe houses report in significant numbers that the family companion animal was also the target of violence in the home. Sometimes the dog, for example, may be threatened, harmed, or killed by an adult to intimidate or psychologically abuse another adult or a child.

- Researchers are not yet sure why or with what degree of certainty, but studies suggest that when a child is abusive toward an animal, that may be a red flag for future violent behavior toward people or a sign that the child is being abused physically, sexually, and/or psychologically.

- In a 2001 study by the Humane Society of the United States, of 1,000 cases of reported animal cruelty nationwide, 20 percent were perpetrated by teenagers.

Here's what you can do for your child and his or her friends:

- Know what to look for. Review the list of dos and don'ts for child behavior toward your dog or any animal. Anything that causes your dog or any animal pain or distress, even if it is not on the list, should also be cause for concern.

· Prevent inappropriate behavior. Study the dos list and encourage your child to follow those behaviors. Be an active kid canine coach, especially where teenagers and their friends are concerned. Intervene and invite the dog into his safety zone if you suspect your child of inappropriate behavior.

· Teach your child empathy for your dog and other animals. Include your child in the care and gentle petting of your dog. Ask your child to imagine how your dog feels, and what things make him feel safe or unsafe. Show your child how your dog demonstrates that he is feeling safe or threatened by using the dog warning signs earlier in this chapter. Demonstrate kindness to animals and model the attitude and actions toward animals you'd like your child to have. Seemingly small acts like putting up a birdfeeder in your yard or helping an animal in need can make a big difference in your child's eyes.

· Actively address any incident of cruel treatment of your dog, whether by your child or a visiting child. It is not normal for a child to hurt, torment, or intentionally cause distress to animals. Children do not do this as part of normal exploration and development. If you witness or hear of even one incident of cruel behavior, you should be concerned. Talk with your child about the incident to find out more about what he was thinking and feeling. Enlist the help of a family or school counselor, teacher, pediatrician, or family doctor.

· Report acts of animal cruelty, abuse, or neglect to your local animal control officer. If you witness a child inflict pain or distress on an animal, notify a school counselor or principal. This is important for the child, and for other children and animals, who may be the next victims of such cruelty.

See the appendix for resources with more information about the link between animal abuse and other violence, and what you can to do help your child and your dog.

Helping Your Child Say Goodbye:
Coping With Loss and Grief

It is often said that the only thing wrong with dogs is that their lives are all too short. Regardless of when or why your dog dies, the death of your dog likely will be a painful and profound experience. For your child, the loss of their dog may be one of their first experiences with death. They will have feelings that may be new to them and they may pose questions to you that are difficult to answer. It may be tempting to try to shield your child from the realities of the experience by using euphemisms or half-truths to answer their questions, which is certainly a normal, understandable impulse. After all, you will be grieving, too, so you'll understand the pain your child is feeling, but it is not advisable to be anything less than truthful. Death is a normal part of life, and lying about it may confuse or frighten your child. Instead, consider some of the following guidelines for helping your child through this difficult experience:

Be honest. It's okay to tell your child that your dog died. It's okay to tell them that it makes you sad. Openness will make it more likely that your child will share his or her feelings with you, too.

Keep it simple. Avoid using euphemisms, such as you had to have your dog "put to sleep" or saying things like your dog "went away." Comments like this can really frighten children, who may confuse being put to sleep with sleeping and bed time, or going away from you with being lost and never coming back. It's best to explain in simple terms that sometimes dogs get very sick or hurt or old, and the time comes when they die. You can reassure your child that you did your best, and the dog doctor did her best, to make your dog well again. But sometimes not even the veterinarian can make a dog stay alive. It is okay to feel sad, angry, lonely, numb, or upset. You may wish to draw from your family's spiritual tradition to help your child accept what has happened.

Include your child in rituals to celebrate your dog's life. Some people find it helpful to cope with grief by planning a ritual or ceremony to remember their dog. Below are some things my clients have found helpful to do when their dogs have died. By discussing it together, you will know what is right for your family.

- Burying the dog together and having a funeral. You may want to write down and read some special memories about your dog. Reading a special poem is a nice idea, too.

- Lighting a candle

- Writing down happy memories of your dog and putting them in a special journal

- Laying a wreath at a favorite spot

- Having a special stone engraved and placing it in the yard together

- Planting a tree in memory of your dog

- Making a donation to a veterinary research fund, animal shelter, or adoption group

- Writing a letter to the dog

- Drawing pictures of the dog

- Creating a shadow box (or deep framed box) with photos and special items, like her collar

Please see the appendix for list of helpful resources and picture books for children and adults. Everyone grieves differently and there's no one "right" way to feel or to go through it. It's always hard to imagine at the time, but one day the incredible sadness of saying goodbye to your four-legged friend gives way to happy memories. When the time is right, you may even decide together to invite another dog into your family.

Frequently Asked Questions about Child-Dog Relationships

"I feel bad not letting the kids and dog play together. I seem to remember doing this all the time when I was young. Why can't I just turn my child and dog loose in the backyard for some good old-fashioned fun?"

I can understand this. We all have an idyllic image of dogs and children playing in the grass, the sun streaming down on them. They all romp around, the kids giggling, the whole scene unfolding in slow motion.

However, to put it bluntly, if real-life were so simple, kids would not be at highest risk for dog bites by their own dogs or their friends' dogs. Consider this analogy: Under the right circumstances, a stove is a wonderful addition to the household. But it takes some proactive parental effort to keep it that way. What would you think about my logic if I said, "I feel bad about not letting the kids play with the stove any way they want"?

Kids who play unattended with dogs learn bad habits about how to treat dogs and are at risk for bites, or worse. Dogs who play unattended learn bad habits and to fear or resent children. In real life, dogs and children can enjoy playing together with the help of a kid canine coach. Choose games that everyone can handle, meaning the children know how to behave around the dog, and the dog remains easily under your verbal control. Keep play sessions short and light, so no one gets overexcited or starts making bad decisions. Choose a structured activity so everyone can be safe together (for some specific ideas, see the games section in this chapter and the appendix). My bet is that they will all have a blast! Think about it like this: Growing up is largely about having fun, learning to be safe, and learning respect and empathy for others. Your kids and your dog can count themselves lucky to have such a competent, caring kid canine coach to guide them.

"What is the safest way for our child to touch our dog?"

Children must learn to pet the dog slowly and gently under the chin or on the side of the face. The chest is good, too. Dogs who snuggle closer for more may then be stroked gently on the side of the body. Most dogs feel uncomfortable when they are touched on the top of the head, the back, or when people reach for them from behind.

Ideally you will prepare your dog to cope with inappropriate touch that may happen unexpectedly. One of my clients did this by giving her dog a quick hug followed by a favorite treat. If your dog backs away or shows other stress signs, use a milder version of the hug to start. For example, face the same direction as your dog and reach only from underneath. Gradually (over several three-minute sessions) make your hug more and more like a real hug. If your dog does not look forward to hugs from you after a couple of sessions, consult with a qualified professional before you proceed. It would be very easy to inadvertently teach your dog to be an annoyed by invasive touch, so I advise working on this under the supervision of a qualified professional.

"How can we keep our child away from dog toys?"

Keep dog toys picked up off the floor. Teach your child never to approach your dog when she has any item, including toys, bones, or any other object your dog might get a hold of, such as a stick, pillow, sock, tissue, or pencil. Your child should learn to seek your help rather than reach for the dog.

"How do we train our dog not to want to run free when he sneaks out the front door? If there is a crack when we open the door for a guest, or if the kids are running in and out of the house and forget to close the door, our dog will bolt and run for about twenty or thirty minutes until one of us tracks him down. He doesn't come when we call, and we have to chase him around the neighborhood to get him back. What can we do to get the dog back?"

Door bolting is an aggravating habit indeed. Trying to fix it is a little like trying to stop a person from running out the door on impulse, even though they are rewarded with gifts and piles of cash every time they do. That's how rewarding it is for your dog. Once your dog is loose on one of these fun-filled romps, it's no time for training. Your dog may even think it's pretty fun having you hunt him down. ("Yay! Now we're all running around the neighborhood playing keep away, yay!") All the come-when-called training in the world won't help if your dog is even occasionally rewarded with the equivalent of a free trip to Disneyland by bolting out the door.

To me the more productive question is: how do you keep the dog from bolting out the door in the first place? Here are some suggestions that my clients have had success with:

- When you're expecting visitors, place your dog in his
  safety zone, in the kitchen behind a baby gate, or in the
  bathroom with the door shut, just long enough for you to
  let the guests in, then let your dog out once the front door
  is shut. When your guests are ready to leave, temporarily
  confine your dog again to prevent him from bolting out
  the door.

- Tie a ribbon or a bandanna to the inside doorknob. This serves as a strong visual reminder not to open the door until the dog is securely in the other room or in his safety zone.

- Affix a screen door or a storm door to the outside of the door from which the dog typically escapes. This can be a good backup system in case the kids forget to shut the door behind them.

- Keep the door locked. This prevents children and adults from popping in to say hello or to play, which leads to cracking open the door just wide enough for your dog to slip through.

If it seems like a pain to have to make some of these changes, ask yourself whether it's more effort to briefly confine the dog, or to drop everything you're doing to spend a half hour trying to catch your dog as he runs wild through the neighborhood. Most people agree it's much easier and less stressful to use prevention. Prevention also allows you to have better success in teaching your dog to come when you call, since you can better control what your dog finds rewarding and associate that with coming to you. Also bear in mind that dogs who run loose usually run into trouble eventually. They may be hit by a car, frighten someone, get into a tangle with another dog or wild animal, harass cats and other animals, bite a child, or be reported to animal control by annoyed neighbors.

If your dog should get loose before you have a chance to implement these prevention strategies, do not chase him. Chasing your dog just makes matters worse. Run the opposite direction he is going, cheering and clapping as though you're having the time of your life. When he catches up, avoid trying to grab him. You won't be able to pull it off, and the attempt will only get him charging around again. Instead, let him nibble on some treats (ideally you brought real meat outside with you), and while he does, ever so casually and slowly, reach underneath his chin with your free hand and gently take hold of the collar. Don't let go. Walk all the way back to the house like this. Go inside, close the door, then give him the rest of the meat. Then let go of the collar. Finally, pledge on your dog's safety and your own sanity to prevent this pandemonium in the future.

"Our dog is friendly, but she's very big. We're afraid our toddler is going to get whacked in the face with that gigantic tail of hers. Is there anything we can do?"

If your dog and child are close together and you imagine an impending tail lashing, the fastest way to intervene is to ask your dog to perform a behavior that will prevent it.

There are several to choose from: sit, nose touch (if you're at the right angle), back up, down, move over (you can get fancy and teach each direction, so with one word you can get your dog to move laterally right or left), and stop (or stand) would all be handy. The most efficient way to teach these would be to get a trainer to show you. It really doesn't take long to master a couple of these if you practice about five minutes each day. You could always attempt to scoop your child out of the way in these situations, but I think it's preferable that the dog demonstrate impulse control and body awareness around the more vulnerable child. Before long, your child will be able to cue your dog to sit when she wants the dog to stop moving.

"A wagging tail means the dog is feeling friendly and it's okay to interact with him, right?"

It is very important to be aware of a dog's body language, since it is one of the best ways to judge how the dog is feeling. However, you may be surprised to learn that relying on a wagging tail as a sign of friendliness has gotten many a person bitten. My colleagues and I often remark how many bite victims lament that the dog was wagging his tail right before they were bitten.

Why the confusion? Well, imagine someone from the planet Zorg says to you, "A human with their arm extended into the air means they are feeling friendly and it's okay to interact with them, right?" You would reply, "It depends." After all, the human might be waving hello with friendly intent. However, they might just be hailing a cab, or they may be flipping someone the bird! Just an arm in the air is not enough to judge whether it's safe to approach or touch the human.

So it is with dogs. A dog soliciting affection and interaction with a person may well be moving his tail, and in a very specific way: low or level with his back, sweeping back and forth usually in a wide or circular motion, or wiggling low if it is an exceptionally short tail. This is usually accompanied by soft, squinty eye contact, ears flopped back (not pinned back or held stiffly halfway back), and curvy body postures. In such a case, the dog will usually approach the person and seek out touch. However, a dog who is moving his tail, but with the tail held stiffly, high above his back, is indicating arousal at a minimum and possibly an offensive posture. If the tail is held up, totally still or moving back and forth like a flag, and the dog is stiff and focused, usually with his ears held forward, do not approach him. He could be warning you he is ill at ease and preparing for offensive movements. A dog moving his tail while it's tucked between his legs is also ill at ease, even if it's just nervousness, and it is best not to approach. Look for a low, wiggly tail and body and wait for the dog to approach you, not the other way around. And, of course, there are all of the subtle warning signs of stress that we have discussed, which can help you interpret what that moving tail might mean.

Chapter 4:
The Other Dogs in Your Child's Life

Rules for Visiting Friends, Relatives, and Neighbors Who Have Dogs

Suppose your child is going to visit neighbors, in-laws, or grandparents who have a dog. If you're with your child during the visit, that's an excellent opportunity to be a kid canine coach away from home. Reinforce your child's appropriate behavior around the dog. Watch the dog for any warning signs; don't assume the dog's owners will do this. Should you see any warning signs, or if your child is getting a bit rambunctious, over-tired, or having trouble listening, it's time for you to spring into action. Guide your child away from the dog or ask that the dog be removed to another room. You may also take your child to another room or outdoors to give everyone a break.

If your child is going for a visit without you, a little leg work ahead of time can go a long way to preventing injury, stress, and the development of bad habits. Think of what you would do to prepare your child for making a visit without you in general. You'd probably want to make sure there were some basic safety precautions in place. The same thing applies when you're dealing with dogs. First, you'll want to meet the dog and talk with the adults about how they manage child-dog interactions in their household. Be aware that it doesn't do much good to ask your neighbor or relative, "Is your dog friendly?" "How is your dog with kids?" or "Do you supervise the kids and dog?" A much more useful question would be "Where will your dog be while my daughter is visiting?" Unacceptable answers include, "Oh, Bella loves kids, don't worry," or "We usually have the dog out in the yard during the day," or "The kids can do anything to the dog and he doesn't mind." A kid canine coach would not respond in any of these ways. Better responses include, "I keep the dog in his crate unless the kids are playing very quietly, then I let him out and we all have some time together. If the dog is out of her crate, I make sure the kids pet correctly and that they pet one at a time." Another good response would be, "The dog tends to hang out wherever we are, but how would *you* feel most comfortable?" Then you can decide whether your preference that the dog be kept in another room or in her crate will likely be honored. Think of it like this: your neighbors and relatives have scissors in their houses, probably several pairs, but you wouldn't let your child visit if they left the scissors lying around and permitted the children to run around with them.

One mother told me that her daughter had visited a neighbor who has a dog. The daughter is fearless and can be quite bold with animals. She came home from the visit and reported that the dog had bitten her. It had hurt a little bit and she had cried, but the bite hadn't left a mark. It wasn't at all clear what had occurred just before the bite. Perhaps the dog was an aloof type who had a low threshold for aggression. Perhaps the girl had interacted with him inappropriately.

I recommended that the mother talk with the dog's owner to get more information about what happened before and after the bite. I also felt that she should accompany her daughter to the neighbor's house on the next visit. The girl needed to be coached on how to behave safely around dogs. That would also give the mother a chance to express her preference that the dog be kept elsewhere when her daughter visited.

Most people don't pay too much attention to these issues until there's an injury. That's one reason why dog bites to children by the family dog and friends' dogs are so common. We just assume things will be fine, and then we're surprised when there's a bite. Why wait for this to happen to your child? Be proactive and keep both your child and your dog on the right track.

Rules for Meeting Unfamiliar Dogs out in the World

Once, after I had taken one of our dogs to the veterinarian, I was sitting in the waiting room with my dog while the bill was being calculated. Two boys approached us, their mother right behind them, and the older one, about six years old, made a beeline for my dog. His mother said nothing to the boys, so I extended my hand, palm held out in a stop gesture, smiled, and said, "Wait. Do you know the rule? You should always ask permission before you pet a dog." The mother said nothing. The boy, not missing a beat, replied, "But I have a dog who looks just like that!" The mother remained silent. I said, "Well, that's great. I bet you enjoy your dog a lot. But you don't know this dog, and he might be afraid or in pain. A dog might bite when he feels that way. Today is not a good day to pet him, I'm afraid." I was looking out for the child's well-being as well as my dog's comfort.

Not all dog owners know what to do when a child approaches their dog. Just think how much less stress and injury there would be if all dog handlers and parents made this a priority. It's very important to teach your child what to do when he sees a dog he'd like to pet. Here are the rules for the right way to greet a dog:

- Breed, color, and familiarity are not reliable indicators that a dog is safe to pet.

- Children and adults must always ask permission before approaching any dog, even a familiar one.

- Teach your child to look at the dog's owner or at the dog's paw, rather than staring at the dog's eyes, while asking for permission to pet the dog.

This child has asked her guardian and the dog's owner for permission to pet the dog, and both have said yes. The child does not stare at the dog, but rather stands at an angle and pets under the chin and on the upper chest. Notice the dog is leaning towards the child for more. Photo by author.

Happy Kids, Happy Dogs

- If permission is granted by the owner, your child should stand sideways with relaxed arms hanging down at his sides.

- Do not extend your hand for the dog to sniff. This is a threatening gesture and can invite a bite.

- If the dog does not approach you to initiate an interaction, do not move toward or touch the dog. Instead, admire the dog from afar and ask the owner about him.

- If the dog approaches, the best way to touch most dogs is with gentle strokes on the side of the face and under the chin. Do not pat the top of the head.

- Do not extend your hand toward, stare at, lean over, hug, or kiss any dog.

- Only one person should pet the dog at a time. When there are several children present, they must wait their turn; this goes for adults, too.

Never approach a dog who is unattended, even just to look at him or talk to him. This includes dogs who are left in a car or tied up outside of a restaurant or store. Just recently I saw a mother holding her child's hand, going up to a dog who was tied outside of a grocery store. The mother was smiling and clearly just wanted her daughter to take an interest in the dog, but what she was inadvertently modeling for the child was the assumption that it is okay to approach an unattended dog. It's not. Just because someone leaves their dog unattended does not mean the dog is friendly. On the contrary, the dog may be more stressed than usual since he's been left by his owner.

When you are out with your dog or when visitors come to your home, remember that most people don't know the proper way to greet a dog. Before you permit the interac-

Nice to smell you

Dogs have powerful noses and can smell you readily; there's no need to approach or extend your hand. Many dog behavior experts consider the advice to "let a dog sniff you first" to be outdated now that we know so much more about dog body language.

tion, show them what to do with their body, their eyes, and their hands. Take your time. Identify and respect your dog's stress and warning signs. Don't ever force an interaction. If the person does not follow your instructions or your dog is showing warning signs, do not wait to see what happens next. Immediately and cheerfully say, "Fido, come!" or "touch!" and physically take your dog out of the situation. You can then explain to the person that your dog is feeling tired or whatever excuse comes to mind, but don't just wait and watch. Dog bites can happen very, very fast.

These rules for meeting a dog apply to adults, too, not only out of concern for your own safety and the dog's well-being, but because a child may be watching. Children learn a lot about how to behave by watching adults, so it is important to always demonstrate the correct way to greet a dog.

What Your Child Should Do if Approached by a Stray Dog

At a recent hospital presentation, I explained to the audience that the majority of dog bites are to children and are inflicted by the family dog or a neighbor's dog. In fact, I quipped, it's not as though kids are being bitten by stray dogs as they stand at the school bus stop. I told the audience that such occurrences are very rare (which is true), but wouldn't you know it? The very next day, the local newspaper ran a front-page story about how a dog attacked two children as they were waiting for the school bus. The story said that the dog had been repeatedly biting a small boy, and that an older girl had tried to pull the dog away by the collar to save the boy. Even though the girl sustained bites on both arms, she hung on to the dog in an effort to protect the small boy until the bus happened to pull up and the driver was able to scare the dog off.

This bus stop incident must have been terribly frightening for everyone involved. It might also have been prevented if a dog with such a volatile temperament had not been allowed to run loose, and if the parents of the children at the bus stop had taught them what to do if approached by a stray dog. The little boy was quoted as saying the dog started out playing with him, but the play soon turned "serious." The two things that immediately occurred to me were: "That was not a safe dog to have loose in the neighborhood," and "Why is a child playing with a stray dog?" The adults, both the dog's owner and the child's parents, could potentially have prevented the injuries. Because not everyone owns friendly dogs, and because dogs sometimes get loose and out of control, it is important to teach children how to keep safe when you're not around to protect them.

Dogs sometimes get loose. Unfortunately, your child may encounter a stray dog one day. Teach your child ahead of time what to do to avoid a bite. A study in Australia showed that even weeks after children were taught what to do when encountering a stray dog, all but one child remembered how to apply their lesson. Taking a proactive approach is especially important if your child is very comfortable with your family dog. Such a comfort level could make your child more likely to interact with a stray dog, which is not advisable.

Instead, when confronted by a stray dog, your child should pretend he is a tree, with his arms folded across his chest. A tree stands up tall, makes no sounds, no eye contact, and no movements. Your child should be perfectly still and quiet, looking down at his shoes. The dog may sniff, bark, touch, lick, or nip your child, but your child's best reaction to avoid injury is to remain standing still like a tree. Many dogs will investigate and then move along, but talking, yelling, running, or trying to hide may arouse the dog and even lead to a bite or mauling. When your child thinks the dog is gone, they should count to ten and then quietly walk to tell an adult about the dog. It helps to keep things as simple as possible when explaining the safety rules to your child:

If a dog rushes up to your child, she should pretend to be a tree by folding her arms and looking down at her shoes.
Photo courtesy of Celeste Huntington.

1. If a dog appears, whether you know the dog or not, pretend to be a tree.

2. Fold your arms, stand still, be quiet, look at your shoes.

3. When the dog goes away, count to ten, then quietly walk to tell an adult.

Should your child be knocked down by a dog, or fall down, he should pretend to be a rock. This means staying on the ground face down, drawing his knees up to his chest, and using his arms to cover the sides of his face and ears until the dog goes away. Rocks are very still and quiet, so that is how your child should be.

I recommend practicing with your own dog present and with a couple of friendly neighbor dogs until it comes easily to your child. The helper dog will likely just mill around, but it will help simulate a real-life incident for your child. Think of it like a fire drill; you may not need it but you'll be glad you practiced.

If your child is knocked down, he should pretend to be a rock by tucking his knees to his chest and covering his head, ears, face, and neck with his arms and hands.
Photo by Ginger Long.

What to Do if Your Child Is Afraid of Dogs

At some point, your child, or a child you know, may be reluctant to approach your dog. Please do not force the child to move closer than he or she wants to and certainly do not permit your dog to rush up to the child, whether he's a friendly dog or not. This may mean using a leash indoors for a time to better control your dog's whereabouts. If forced to be in close proximity with dogs, your fearful child could become increasingly anxious around them. Not only that, the dogs in question could become anxious about being faced with a freaked-out child.

I once had a neighbor whose children loved to watch us walk our dog. One of the children liked to pet the dog, but the other, a five-year-old boy, was quite hesitant. He felt comfortable watching his sister pet the dog, but preferred to watch from about four feet away. We would smile and chat with the kids and their mother, and then be on our way. This approach allowed the boy to gain confidence at his own pace. He gradually started coming closer, asking questions about the dog, and sometimes even stood close enough to touch him.

One day, the boy's father witnessed his son's reluctance. He told the boy in a firm voice, "Now, we can't have you being afraid of dogs," as he literally picked the boy off his feet

Don't force it

Some parents worry that their fearful child is at risk around dogs because dogs can "smell fear." I know of no evidence to support this notion. In fact, it is by forcing an interaction that the parent is likely contributing to their child's fear and possibly inappropriate, even risky, behavior around dogs.

and tried to position him closer to me and my dog. Understandably, the boy panicked. The boy's face was filled with sheer terror. He struggled and nearly started to cry as he protested, "No! No!" Who could blame him? How would you like it if somebody pushed you within inches of a snake to force you to get over your fear?

This is not the way to go, unless you want your child to go from cautious to panicked at the sight of dogs. Instead, arrange interactions only with dogs you know, who are gentle and unlikely to charge or jump. Sometimes smaller dogs intimidate children less, so if you know someone with a smaller dog, that might be a good choice. (Just make sure you don't choose a puppy, because they can sometimes be the most rambunctious and mouthy.) Let the child go at his own pace and he'll likely come to feel pleasant and re-laxed in the presence of dogs. Your child should ask permission to pet the dog anyway, so you'll know when he's ready. I'll take a calm, steady, cautious child around dogs any day over a fearless, inappropriate one. Which child do you think is more likely to be aware of the dog's feelings and behavior? Which child do you think is likelier to be bitten?

By the way, you may be interested to know how I handled the above situation. As soon as the boy's father lifted up his son and the boy wailed, I did three things. First, I smiled at my dog and cheerfully encouraged him to take two giant steps away from the boy and his father. This showed the dog that stressed-out children are a tip-off for feeling calm and safe, and that my dog could look to me for guidance if something new or confusing happened. This beats leaving the dog to worry and take matters into his own hands (or teeth). Second, I smiled at the little boy and said, "It's okay to just look at the dog. Isn't he beautiful? I think his coat is so fluffy. And his paws are really cute, that's my favorite." Third, while I talked, I signaled the dog to lie down, so that he got smaller from the boy's perspective. The boy, now standing on his own two feet, relaxed and chatted with me about the dog. Then I said we'd see them later, and my dog and I moved away. Stick to your child's comfort level and you won't need to coordinate so many details. Should he become worried, remain upbeat and create more space from the dog.

How to Choose the Right Dog for Your Family

If you don't have a dog now, but are thinking about adding a dog to your family, first consider the following: Get a dog because you and your partner want one. Don't get a dog because your child wants one. A child cannot and should not be the dog's main caretaker. Helping with doggie chores all takes place under the guidance of the kid canine coach (you), so getting a dog will mean lot of extra work for all of you. You will also have a lot of extra fun. Just remember that you, not your child, are responsible for the dog's daily care. Regardless of the promises your child makes, or the rules you attempt to put in place, you will be the one who has to take care of the dog's daily needs for affection, training, exercise, and feeding.

If you already have a dog and are thinking about getting another one, be aware that having two dogs is more than twice the work of having one. Don't get a dog just because you feel guilty you're not spending enough time with the dog you have now. Another dog is no substitute for your care and affection. Keep in mind that the new dog and your current dog may not always get along, or they may ignore each other much of the time.

You'll also have to make arrangements for leash-walking two dogs, car-riding for two dogs, adding another safety zone, and training to get your new dog up to speed, especially since the new dog may have unexpected behavior problems. If you just want more canine action, consider taking an agility, tracking, or Rally-O class or finding a day camp for your child and your dog.

What if your child is just going to burst, they're so desperate to have a dog?

Your child won't burst. They are counting on you to create a sane, happy, safe environment for them, so hold your ground if it's not yet the right time to get a dog. There are lots of ways to get your child interacting with and enjoying dogs until they are old enough to have one as part of the family. When I was growing up, I was nearly obsessed with having a dog, but my family moved internationally quite frequently, and complying with quarantine laws at the time would have been grueling for a dog. Looking back, I also think that my parents realized they had their hands full with two young children, and that adding a dog into the mix too soon would have been too much for everyone.

Here are some ideas for satisfying your young dog enthusiast until the time is right to get a dog of your own. You'll notice some are geared toward older children, some for very young ones.

- picture books and coloring books featuring dogs (see the appendix for some ideas)

- collecting dog stickers

- creating arts and crafts with dog themes

- playing with dog puppets of different breeds (it might also be fun to make your own together)

- dog stories to read to your child or for them to read on their own (see the appendix for ideas)

- visiting with friends' dogs

- volunteering at an animal shelter or packing up items to donate to the animal shelter

- shadowing a veterinarian or dog trainer for "career day" at school

- helping a neighbor train their dog.

What if you're sure you want a dog?

If, having considered all of this, all the adults in the family are truly excited about getting a dog (and your child is, too), don't make another move until you do the following:

1. Read the guidelines for selecting your new animal companion at www.openpaw.org. The questions this website poses will help you figure out the right dog for you. (Amazingly, it's free.) You'll also find state-of-the-art information on preparing for the new dog or puppy and what to do after you bring him home.

2. Read both of these books: *Paws to Consider* and *Successful Dog Adoption* (see the appendix for more information). These books should be required reading for any prospective dog or puppy owner. Regardless of where you get your dog you'll need up-to-date information on breeds and breed mixes, and on specifically what to do to select your dog. While you're reading, bear in mind that just because a breed is popular, low-shedding, or renowned for being good with kids does not mean that individual dogs of that breed will be right for you.

Happy Kids, Happy Dogs

3. Wait until your youngest child is at least five years old. Having a new dog is almost like having an infant in terms of time commitment and sleep deprivation. No one truly grasps this until they are up to their eyeballs in stress, and they are asking, "What was I thinking? Why didn't anyone try to stop me!?"

I also strongly recommend you get professional help with your dog search. No one thinks they could end up with a dog with an unmanageable behavior problem. But nowadays it happens all the time, to people just like you, who have done what they thought was best to find a new dog. The Centers for Disease Control and Prevention and the American Veterinary Medical Association, as well as the national organizations Dog Bite Law and Open Paw all recommend that any person planning on adding a dog to their household first consult with a professional.

The idea of getting professional assistance when selecting the best dog possible is a cutting-edge concept that you may not have considered before. When potential dog owners first hear that I offer this service (which I developed at the urging of a veterinarian who had become concerned by all of the behavior problems she saw in her clients' new dogs and puppies), they wonder how the service can benefit them. I often hear things like: "We've had a dog before; we know what to do." "I've had this breed all my life." "We've read books and talked with breeders." "The shelter/rescue group/breeder said that they temperament-test their dogs." "I know a friendly dog when I see one."

Unfortunately, many puppy and dog owners have said these same things, but later wished they had gotten professional advice from the beginning after they've experienced one or more of the following:

- Their dog bit someone within days of the adoption or purchase.

- Their dog began threatening family members or visitors within a few weeks after the adoption or purchase.

- Their dog did not get along with the other animals in the household.

- Their dog became out of control whenever he saw another dog out on a leash walk.

- The family was ready to get a dog, but the particular dog they chose turned out to have requirements far beyond what the family could manage.

· The dog they chose showed aggression towards children.

· The breed they chose did not turn out to be what the books or breed enthusiasts promised.

· Their dog started out calm but became increasingly unmanageable.

These things do not have to happen to you. Especially with a child or children in your household, doesn't it make sense to take modern, proactive measures to assure the best fit possible?

Guidelines for finding the best dog for your family

Avoid the three most common pitfalls.

1. Rushing into it. The new dog could ideally be part of your family for ten to fifteen years, which is a huge commitment. Make sure you have the most up-to-date information on what to do. Take your time. Use your mind as well as your heart. You won't regret it.

2. Letting pressure from someone else drive the process. A dog takes a lot of time, energy, money, and emotion to care for properly. Getting one for the wrong reasons, like guilt or pressure, is no way to begin a successful relationship. Remember that children cannot be the dog's primary caretakers, which many adults forget until it is too late and they are smothered in stress.

3. Pity. Getting a dog mainly because you feel sorry for him is not the right way to start a healthy relationship. The dog or puppy you are considering might indeed be the right dog for you, but it's crucial to be sensible in evaluating him, or you could both end up regretting it. Learn what to look for, what to ask, and adopt the dog who would truly be the best fit for both of you.

Seek out a dog who is affiliative toward people.

The most important quality you should look for in a new dog, in terms of avoiding bites to your child or his playmates, is a strong tendency toward affiliative behavior toward people. That means you should only consider adopting or purchasing a dog who actively seeks out affection from people, including strangers and children. Here are some things highly affiliative dogs will do when you meet them:

- The dog should approach you right away without being coaxed, called, sweet-talked, pulled, or bribed with toys or treats. This applies whether you are indoors and outdoors. The right dog should look forward to meeting a new person and come right over.

- The dog should approach you with the tail held level with his back, or slightly lower than back-level. The tail may wag in wide sweeps, back and forth, in a big circle like a propeller, or wiggle back and forth if it's very short. His tail should not be tucked between the legs or raised up above the dog's back. Even dogs with very short or cropped tails show these basic tail positions.

- The dog should hold his ears loosely back or low, and have eyes that are squinty and show a soft, gentle expression.

- The dog should ask to be touched by you by nuzzling you, nudging you, looking at you, lifting a front paw, pressing against you with the front part of his body or shoulder, curving toward you, or jumping up gently and trying to stay up (not just ricocheting off you or body slamming you).

One thing at a time

Don't take your child with you when evaluating dogs or litters of puppies. You will very likely bypass several candidates before settling on one. That one is the dog you'll then want to introduce to your child before making the final decision.

This dog's personality is to be very affiliative with people. Even with a new person, his eyes are squinty and hold a soft expression. His body is curved and wiggly, his tail is level with his back or lower, and he offers sustained contact and gentle licking without being coaxed. Photo by Christopher Sims.

- If you pet the dog, the dog should come closer or nudge to get more petting, not walk away, even one step, or turn his back to you.

- Ideally the dog will be calmed by touch and talking. A dog that gets increasingly wound up the more you engage him is more difficult to have around children, who naturally get excited sometimes.

These guidelines apply to puppies at a breeder's home, puppies or dogs at an animal shelter or foster home, or puppies or dogs at an adoption fair. Factors such as stress, breed, gender, age, time of day, temperature, or the presence of other dogs or cats will not keep a truly friendly, people-oriented dog from connecting with you. Don't let anyone make excuses, and pay no attention if they do. Only if a dog is ill, in pain, or groggy from surgery should less interest in people be excused, and in those cases the dog is clearly not ready to be evaluated.

This dog shows she loves contact with people with her low, sweeping tail wag, her squinty eyes, and her tendency to climb in laps to offer lots of licking. Although she is very big and enthusiastic, she doesn't wildly "kiss and run" or bounce on and off. She keeps a sustained contact and curves, bends, and wiggles her body as she settles into a person's lap. Photo by author.

Be aware that a dog may seem friendly, without in fact being truly interested in connecting with people. Her tongue may be hanging out, her tail going a mile a minute, or she may be moving around looking cute, playing with a toy, another dog, or someone she already knows. These behaviors don't count. These behaviors could describe just about any dog at some point. Watch for specific body language toward you and behaviors that invite you to connect with her. Are the dog's body movements telling you that she wants to make a sustained, gentle connection with you? If the answer is not a resounding "yes," then I recommend continuing your search.

Some of the most respected dog experts in this country agree that this quality of affiliative behavior toward people is key to reducing the likelihood of bites. If potential new dog owners paid attention to this quality when making their choice, I would possibly be out of business. Virtually all of the serious behavior problems I help with would be unlikely to arise, at least not to the degree that they would strain dog-human relationships.

This dog seeks out human contact by approaching with a soft expression, a low and very broadly wagging tail, and ears flopped back. Photo by Christopher Sims.

For more details on why this affiliative quality may help protect you, your child, and your dog, and for step-by-step instructions on how to evaluate dogs you are considering adding to your family, see the best book on this topic: *Successful Dog Adoption* (see the appendix for more information).

Conclusion

Given all the media attention fatal dog attacks receive, you may be worried that your dog and your child could become part of those fatal dog mauling statistics. But what are the chances, statistically speaking, of your child being killed by your dog? The chances are extremely remote. The real question is, what are the chances of your child being bitten by your dog or a neighbor's dog? Unfortunately, the chances are very high.

You want your dog and your child to be friends. You want them to grow up loving, respecting, counting on and playing with each other. You can help make this happen if you remember to do all of the following as your child grows up:

1. Meet your dog's daily needs for exercise, attention, and training so that he won't develop bad habits and so his behavior will shine.

2. Be an effective kid canine coach by teaching your child the dos and don'ts, monitoring your dog for signs of stress, and actively creating pleasant associations for your dog with your child.

3. Use the safety zone when you're too busy or too tired to coach.

All the hard work will be worth it. You'll be preparing your child and your dog for a lifetime of mutual respect and trust. May the friendship between them flourish for years to come!

Kid Canine Quiz: Test Your Knowledge

True or False?

1. T   F

   A wagging tail held high means a dog is feeling friendly.

2. T   F

   If your dog leaves the room when your toddler comes in,
   it's a sign he's learning to feel at ease with the child.

A lot of kid canine coaching went into creating this idyllic scene.
Photo courtesy of Celeste Huntington.

3. T   F

Children should be encouraged to gently hug dogs.

4. T   F

Dogs who are taught to "say please" (by sitting automatically when they want something) learn to control their own impulses and enjoy the benefit of mental exercise.

5. T   F

A growl sometimes means a dog is just talking.

6. T   F

A dog who actively seeks out affection from all people, including kids, is a better choice for a family companion than one who is generally aloof with people.

7. T   F

If a dog plays "keep away" or growls to keep you away from her toy or food, it's important to get professional help right away.

8. T   F

It's okay to let the dog sniff the baby's feet, even when they first meet.

9. T   F

As long as you meet your dog's daily needs, it's a good idea to use the safety zone whenever you can't actively coach the child and dog through an interaction.

10. T   F

As long as you supervise your child and dog, they should be fine.

Here are the answers, followed by the page numbers that explain the answer fully.

1. False. (131, 147, 148)
2. False. (83)
3. False. (79)
4. True. (34, 42)
5. False. (1, 82, 84, 120)
6. True. (89, 145–148)
7. True. (14, 71)
8. True. (63, 65)
9. True. (20)
10. False. (4, 108, 109, 120)

Appendix A:
Resources to Prepare Your Child and
Dog for Success

This list includes books and videos that advocate dog-friendly training methods and correct child-dog behavior. All are available through amazon.com and/or dogwise.com. I have omitted some popular choices if they don't prepare children and dogs for success (for example, one otherwise useful book I've omitted gives instructions for wrestling with the dog and recommends an unsafe way for children to meet dogs).

The best books designed for children are:

Meeting Milo and Meeting Milo Workbook by Yvette Van Veen and David J. Perks (a picture book that makes learning about dog safety easy and fun, designed for ages three through six)

Puppy Training for Kids by Sarah Whitehead (a beautiful, thorough, and concise training book, designed for ages four through twelve)

Dog Safety for Parents and Children

Doggone Safe
www.doggonesafe.com

Provides tips and activities for kids and dogs. Features the two most important things to teach your kids.

Centers for Disease Control and Prevention:
National Dog Bite Prevention Week: www.cdc.gov/ncipc/duip/biteprevention.htm

Preventing parasite & disease transmission from dogs to humans: www.cdc.gov/healthypets/resources/brochures.htm

Offers studies, statistics, and prevention strategies.

American Society of Plastic Surgeons: Dog Bite Awareness:
www.plasticsurgery.org/public_education/Dog-Bite-Awareness.cfm

Provides facts, prevention strategies, and activity sheets for kids.

National Association for Humane and Environmental Education:
www.nahee.org/bite.asp

Provides board games, posters, classroom lesson plans, and coloring books.

Learning to Read Dog Body Language

What Is My Dog Thinking: The Essential Guide to Understanding Pet Behavior by Gwen Bailey

Know Your Dog: An Owner's Guide to Dog Behavior by Bruce Fogle

Calming Signals: What Your Dog Tells You (video/DVD) by Turid Rugaas

Body Language: What do you see?: www.diamondsintheruff.com/bodylang1.html

This website allows you to practice identifying the subtleties of dog body language depicted in each photo. You can drag your cursor over the photo to see a description and interpretation of the dog's body language.

Preparing for Baby

Look for a motorized crawling baby doll at a toy store near you (about $15).

CDs of baby and child sounds: www.hanaleipets.com

Food puzzle toys for dogs, treats, training gear, baby gates and exercise pens: www.pet-expertise.com, www.sit-stay.com

Reading for Youngsters that Features Correct Child-Dog Interactions

Flip through books before you buy. Does the story encourage respect and empathy for others, including dogs? If so, that's a good sign. Do the illustrations depict incorrect or unsafe gestures toward dogs? If so, consider titles like these instead:

Baby books

Touch and Feel Pets by Nicola Deschamps (not to be confused with Touch & Feel Puppy, which teaches the baby to reach for the dog's toy and the dog's nose)

Board books for toddlers

Doggies by Sandra Boynton

Puppy Playtime a Golden Fuzzy Book

The Dog: From Arf! Arf! to Zzzzz by The Dog Artlist Collection

Animal Babies around the House by Vicky Weber

Wiggle by Doreen Cronin and Scott Menchin (illustrator)

Preschool

Peek-a-Pet by Marie Torres Cimarusti and Stephanie Peterson (illustrator)

Where's Spot? (series) by Eric Hill

Picture books

Walter the Farting Dog (series) by William Kotzwinkle

Curious George (series) by H. A. Rey

Where the Wild Things Are by Maurice Sendak

Otto Goes to School by Todd Parr

My Big Dog by Susan Stevens Crummel and Janet Stevens (illustrator)

Dog Training

There are hundreds of dog training books and videos on the market. The ones I've listed here teach the most modern, effective, dog-friendly techniques. I've included a range of prices to choose from. All are available through mainstream retailers or www.dogwise. com.

Focus on puppies

Taking Care of Puppy Business by Leslie Nelson and Gail Pivar

Puppy Primer by Brenda Scidmore & Patricia McConnell

The Perfect Puppy: How to Raise a Well-Behaved Dog by Gwen Bailey

Focus on training for any age dog

Management Magic by Leslie Nelson and Gail Pivar

The Power of Positive Dog Training by Pat Miller

Beginning Family Dog Training by Patricia McConnell

The How of Bow Wow by Virginia Broitman and Sherri Lippman (video/DVD)

Focus on changing a problem behavior

The Bark Stops Here by Terry Ryan

The Cautious Canine: How to Help Dogs Conquer their Fears by Patricia McConnell

Dogs are from Neptune: Candid Answers to Urgent Questions about Aggression and Other Aspects of Dog Behavior by Jean Donaldson

Teaching Tricks

The Everything Dog Training and Tricks Book by Gerilyn J. Bielakiewicz

This book offers many tricks from beginner to advanced, family dog tricks, multiple-dog tricks, and creative retrieving tricks (like teaching your dog to bring you a tissue when you sneeze!).

Agility Tricks for Improved Attention, Flexibility and Confidence by Donna Duford

Despite the title, this book requires no equipment or previous experience. There are about ten tricks, including tips on advanced versions of them.

Choosing a New Dog

Successful Dog Adoption by Sue Sternberg

This book covers what to know before looking for a dog online or at a shelter. It also provides step-by-step instructions on what to do when you meet dogs and puppies and how to smoothly integrate the dog or puppy into your household, including housetraining and basic obedience instructions. A must read, no matter where you get your dog.

Paws to Consider: Choosing the Right Dog for You and Your Family by Brian Kilcommons and Sarah Wilson

This book provides honest descriptions of many breeds, mixed breeds, and what you should know before you start looking. You might be surprised.

Open Paw (www.openpaw.org)

This website has valuable guidelines for selecting your new animal companion, which will help you figure out your ideal dog. There are also resources to help with planning for a new dog and what to do once you get her home.

Coping with the Loss of Your Dog

Goodbye, Friend by Gary Kowalksi

When a Pet Dies by Fred Rogers (designed for ages three through eight, though in typical Mr. Rogers fashion, it contains profound insights anyone may find helpful)

The Fall of Freddie the Leaf by Leo Buscaglia (a story about the cycle of life and death for all ages)

A web link with some good basic information about euthanasia and grief is: http://web.vet.cornell.edu/public/petloss/

The Studies Mentioned In This Book

Chapman, S., J. Cornwall, J. Righetti, and L. Sung. "Preventing Dog Bites in Children: Randomised Controlled Trial of an Educational Intervention." *British Medical Journal* (2000) 320: 1512–13.

Hare, B., M. Brown, C. Williamson, and M. Tomasello. "The Domestication of Social Cognition in Dogs." *Science* (2002) 298 (5598): 1634-36.

Hare B., and M. Tomasello. "Human-like Social Skills in Dogs?" *Trends in Cognitive Sciences* (2005) 9 (9): 439–44.

American Veterinary Medical Association Task Force on Canine Aggression and Human-Canine Interactions. "A community approach to dog bite prevention." *Journal of the American Veterinary Medical Association* (2001) 218: 1732–49.

Office of Statistics and Programming, National Center for Injury Prevention and Control, CDC. "Nonfatal Dog Bite-Related Injuries Treated in Hospital Emergency Departments, United States, 2001." *Morbidity and Mortality Weekly Report* (2003) 52 (26): 605–10.

Appendix B:
Where to Seek Help if Your Dog's
Behavior Troubles You

Your veterinarian should be prepared to provide you with referrals to effective, ethical, courteous dog professionals. Use only dog trainers or behavior consultants who refrain from using any form of pain or intimidation. Call a few consultants and chat with them about your dog's issue. If you think you might like to hire the person, ask for a couple of references and then check them. If they are hesitant to put you in touch with a couple of satisfied clients who've had a similar dog problem as yours, look elsewhere. (To observe client confidentiality, ethical trainers will first get permission before giving out their clients' contact information.)

Please remember, every profession has a range of practitioner, from the very talented to the less skilled, so be selective in your choice and work with someone in whom you have confidence. The following is a list of additional resources you might want to take advantage of during your search:

- Animal Behavior Society Certified Applied Animal Behaviorists: www.animalbehavior.org/Applied/CAAB_directory.html

- Association of Pet Dog Trainers: www.apdt.com

- Board Certified Veterinary Behaviorists: www.veterinarybehaviorists.org/Diplomates.htm

- Certified Pet Dog Trainers: www.ccpdt.com

- International Association of Animal Behavior Consultants: www.iaabc.org/consultant_locator.htm

Free national behavior hotlines:

The San Francisco SPCA Animal Behavior Program: For dog issues, call (415) 901-6646, and one of the trainers will get back to you. For cat issues, call (415) 554-3075.

Denver Dumb Friends League: For dog or cat behavior, call toll-free: 1-877-738-0217.

Appendix C:
Resources on Animal Cruelty and Abuse and Humane Education

If you observe your child attempt to harm or frighten either your dog or another animal, seek out help, even if it only happened once. Please don't wait. Your child is telling you loud and clear he or she needs help. Speak with a trusted pediatrician, teacher, principal, clergy member, or family counselor. Prevent further violence by alerting your principal and animal control if another child has tried to harm an animal. Your local animal welfare organization can tell you what you should do if you observe animal cruelty in your neighborhood. It's important to get others involved to help the animal, the child perpetrating the abuse, and to prevent escalation or spread of the violence.

For more information, please consult these excellent resources:

- American Humane (www.americanhumane.org): Dedicated to protecting both children and animals, provides information and resources on the link between companion animal abuse and child abuse.

- The Humane Society of the United States (www.hsus. org): offers information on what parents should know about their children and companion animals. The Youth Education Division of the HSUS publishes materials that help teachers establish a classroom theme of kindness, respect, and tolerance. For subscription information, contact the National Association for Humane and Environmental Education (NAHEE), at www.nahee.org

- The Latham Foundation (www.latham.org): offers educational materials on the connections between child and animal abuse and other forms of violence.

- National Anti-Vivisection Society (www.navs.org): provides information on the link between violence towards animals and other violence, humane education, alternatives to animal dissection in schools, lists of research articles and books, and a terrific FAQ section.

- Office of Juvenile Justice and Delinquency Prevention (www.ncjrs.org/html/ojjdp/jjbul2001_9_2/contents.html): contains eye-opening information about animal cruelty and who perpetrates it.

Appendix D:
A Brief Word about Kids and Cats

Although I don't specialize in cat behavior, I am asked two things so often by parents I thought I'd address them here. The purpose of this appendix is to dispel the two most common myths about cats that I encounter when talking with expectant parents.

If you are pregnant, you do not automatically need to give up your cat.

Toxoplasmosis, an infection caused by a parasite, is the main worry here. To avoid it, just have somebody else clean out the litter box ("oh, darn!" you say) and practice normal good hygiene, like hand-washing. You are much more likely to be exposed by handling raw meat or by gardening where a cat may have defecated than by interacting with your cat. Well-informed obstetricians agree that pregnancy is no reason to abandon your feline friend. If you have a cat behavior problem on your hands, ask your vet for a referral or see the list of animal behavior professionals (under dog behavior resources) to get help before the baby arrives.

Your cat will not suck the life out of your baby.

This is an old superstition (cats can't get a break). If your cat is extra snuggly and you worry that she might try to sleep in the crib with your child, just put a screen door on the nursery. They even make screens that go over the top of the crib now, but personally, I can't imagine fiddling with such a contraption when the baby is yodeling away in anticipation of the 3 a.m. feeding. A screen door seems like the easiest solution. From what cat experts tell me, it's really more of a peace of mind issue than a matter of avoiding a real threat to your baby. If you still have doubts or concerns, address them now by getting a referral from your veterinarian.

Index

About the Author

Barbara Shumannfang is the founder of Top Notch Dog, Inc., through which she helps families prevent, recognize, and modify problem behaviors in their companion dogs. At Duke University Health System and the University of North Carolina Hospitals, she teaches a prenatal seminar on reducing stress and injury in child-dog interactions. She holds a Ph.D. from Duke University in a non-doggy field and is a member of the Association of Pet Dog Trainers and the International Association of Animal Behavior Consultants.

A portion of the proceeds from the sales of this book will be donated to non-profit programs that help at-risk children and shelter dogs. For more information please visit www.topnotchdog.com.

Photo by Christopher Sims

LaVergne, TN USA
22 October 2009
161752LV00011B/46/A